C000247038

RUDOLF STEINER (1861–1925) called his spiritual philosophy 'anthroposophy', meaning 'wisdom of the human being'. As a highly developed seer, he based his work on direct knowledge and perception of spiritual dimensions. He initiated a modern and universal 'science of spirit', accessible to anyone willing to exercise clear and unprejudiced thinking.

From his spiritual investigations Steiner provided suggestions for the renewal of many activities, including education (both general and special), agriculture, medicine, economics, architecture, science, philosophy, religion and the arts. Today there are thousands of schools, clinics, farms and other organizations involved in practical work based on his principles. His many published works feature his research into the spiritual nature of the human being, the evolution of the world and humanity, and methods of personal development. Steiner wrote some 30 books and delivered over 6000 lectures across Europe. In 1924 he founded the General Anthroposophical Society, which today has branches throughout the world.

Also available:

(Esoteric)
Alchemy
Christian Rozenkreutz
The Druids
The Goddess
The Holy Grail

(Practical Applications)
Agriculture
Architecture
Art
Education
Eurythmy
Medicine
Religion
Science
Social and Political Science

(Festivals)
Christmas
Easter
Michaelmas
St John's
Whitsun

RUDOLF STEINER

ATLANTIS

The Fate of a Lost Land and
its Secret Knowledge

Compiled with an introduction,
commentary and notes by
Andrew Welburn

Sophia Books

Sophia Books
An imprint of Rudolf Steiner Press
Hillside House, The Square
Forest Row, East Sussex
RH18 5ES

www.rudolfsteinerpress.com

Published by Rudolf Steiner Press 2001
Reprinted 2007

For earlier English publications of extracted material see p. 103

The material by Rudolf Steiner was originally published in German
in various volumes of the 'GA' (*Rudolf Steiner Gesamtausgabe* or
Collected Works) by Rudolf Steiner Verlag, Dornach. This
authorized edition is published by permission of the Rudolf Steiner
Nachlassverwaltung, Dornach (for further information see p. 106)

All translations revised by Christian von Arnim

A catalogue record for this book is available from the British Library

ISBN 978 185584 194 9

Cover by Andrew Morgan
Typeset by DP Photosetting, Aylesbury, Bucks.
Printed and bound in Great Britain by Cromwell Press Limited,
Trowbridge, Wilts.

Contents

Introduction: Atlantis and Prehistory — A Modern Perspective

by Andrew J. Welburn

What do we really know about human prehistory? What were our remoter ancestors like, the brutish 'cavemen' of popular mythology or, as seems increasingly to be suggested, human but strangely different from ourselves? More and more such questions are being asked. Despite the efforts of generations of fossil-hunters and archaeologists, leading experts on the subject are increasingly driven to admit that much which is essential to understanding the origins and early development of humanity remains an enigma.

Darwin's hope that the emergence of human intelligence could be explained from the gradual animal evolution of uprightness in apes — freeing the hands and arms, leading to tool-making, leading to co-operation and socialization, in turn requiring greater brain-power, and so producing higher intelligence — long dominated the scientific debate about prehistory. Only from the late 1960s did the evidence of new discoveries finally force scientists themselves to question it.[1] Now huge uncertainties and divergencies of opinion have emerged. Rather than a gradual animal development, over 15 million years or so, many now think the evidence indicates more sudden processes (at least in evolutionary terms).

Just the latest phase of the emergence of *Homo* produced a tripling of the brain-size—the 'run-away brain' as some experts call it: an evolutionary leap which now looks less like a product of early human evolution than a force which actively empowered it.[2] Increasingly the scientists have had to ask whether such distinctively human things as language, consciousness, memory are really the results, the by-products as Darwin supposed, of our physical evolution. Was it not rather language, as many have now come to think, which transformed the evolutionary potential of humans and brought about the massive enlargement of brain-power, rather than vice versa? Was it not the closely related factor of social interaction rather than Darwinian competitive hunting activity which drove the emergence of human culture?[3]

The turn-around of cart and horse, so to speak, in the understanding of evolution has once again brought the issue of the human, rather than animal, to the forefront of our thinking. Yet paradoxically, the new trend leaves us with greater chasms to be spanned. It leaves the hominids prior to those breakthrough leaps, whose remains are now being uncovered in greater numbers, looking markedly less human. Sometimes we have the strange phenomenon of closely related hominid types, but the one 'robust' and animal-like, the other 'gracile' and human in tendency. And how are we to explain the extraordinary rate of change shown in human evolution?[4] It is hard to avoid the impression that something is still missing from the picture—that we need a change of perspective still more radical, a deeper insight into our humanity, if we are really to understand what is going on.

Of course it is still a huge leap from these questions to the perspective of Rudolf Steiner — perhaps of the order of an evolutionary breakthrough in our thinking itself! But it is certainly true that, on the basis of his spiritual conception of humanity ('anthroposophy', 'wisdom of man') Rudolf Steiner had already thought through many of the issues now facing research into these fascinating domains. If his Atlanteans still seem far removed from the speculations of the fossil-scientists of today, it must at least be admitted that the appearance, relatively far back, of such things as language, relatively complete and elaborate, rather than as the result of indeterminately long evolutionary chipping, makes the existence of 'human' ways of life in those ancient times something with which we now have to come to terms. And such 'human' features must nevertheless have co-existed with the absence of many of the aspects of human cultural, and even physical evolution, which we now take for granted. The situation Steiner describes of a humanity that had highly developed memory, and dreamlike spiritual perception of their living environment, but nothing of what we know as rationality or self-awareness, makes sense when we abandon the old notion of all human faculties emerging slowly together. Quite different states of development, quite different kinds of consciousness must have existed in the ages of human evolution. Our perspective on ourselves must change accordingly. Knowledge of the Atlantean stage of human development was important to Steiner for precisely this reason, as a part of our understanding of human evolution overall. We need to understand it so as to know how we became human, the nature of our consciousness — and this is crucially important because it is only by seeing how we got here that we can also appreciate our potential for further development. Other modes of human life have existed, and in the future will again be possible. It is this evolutionary perspective which is crucial to Steiner's anthroposophical approach. And the way evolution turns out to have been driven by such factors as language-development, socialization, etc. falls into place for him as part of an idea of evolution that from the very beginning included such 'spiritual' aspects, helping to determine the direction of organic evolution rather than emerging piece-meal from it. We shall see how they figure in his account of the way that 'spiritual evolution' has played into and all along been part of physical evolution, at the human stage bringing about the implanting of memory, language and thought.[5] Despite the huge gulfs that still remain, the con-vergences of approach between spiritual and scientific are also striking, and in many ways Steiner seems to furnish exactly that other half of the equation which was felt to be implied, however enigmatically, by the missing dimension in ordinary scientific thought.

Steiner's Atlanteans are also a timely reminder of the way that our own evolution is always part of a larger evolution — that with a certain stage of development goes a whole world, an ecology of which we are part. With their 'human' but still undifferentiated, 'cosmic' consciousness, they were in touch with the kinetic and growth forces in nature in a direct way which we can no longer experience, except through special techniques and training. It is really only in recent times, with the highly individualistic consciousness we now possess, that it has been possible to forget our interdependence. And it has been the task of spiritual thought, like Rudolf Steiner's, to remind us of the potentialities and also the dangers inherent in this situation. The catastrophe of Atlantis is in part a warning for us today which can only be more urgently addressed to our modern civilization than when Steiner expressed it in these essays and lectures. But there is much more of the positive side, which we also need today, where Rudolf Steiner describes how the consciousness of the Atlanteans concerning the hidden dimensions of the forces of nature was preserved in its essentials in the esoteric thought and practices of the ancient Mysteries. In so far as it thus came down and played a part in Christianity (even if the Church today has forgotten or denied its connections with the Mysteries) it provides us with a key to the role that Christianity can again play in healing the ecological situation of our own day.

What the Mysteries preserved, according to Steiner, was not just a tradition about those primordial times. They preserved a way of entering once again into the 'primitive' consciousness, in touch with the powers of nature, which is still there from our Atlantean heritage, though it has been overlaid by many subsequent layers of development. As a result of their techniques something, at least, of the world of Atlantis could be brought to life again. We have here the clue as to how the Mysteries could hand down knowledge of times so misty and remote, from times when even the disposition of the continents on the earth's surface was different. Every configuration of human development implies the whole world which belonged to it. Therefore to recreate that configuration inwardly is, if done sufficiently deeply and objectively, to rediscover the 'cosmic memory' of those lost times (the Akashic Record as it is sometimes called). Staying in touch with their prehistoric heritage was in fact one of the primary functions of the ancient Mystery-cults, and in them images of the distant past were expressed subsequently by the initiates in myth and vision. Rudolf Steiner thus helps us to understand how humanity's connection with former dispositions of the earth could live on — and can indeed be rediscovered by independent spiritual research today.[6]

As for the changing continents and the riddle of Atlantis itself, Steiner's account has little connection with the efforts of those who would look for evidence in shallow seas that might have been land in historical times, or on the Atlantic ridge. His claim that the changing shapes of continents and oceans are an expression of the constantly moving 'inner life' of the earth rather looks forward once more to advanced ideas of 'continental drift', scientifically mocked and disparaged even long after Steiner's day when they were put forward by Wegener and others, but nowadays central to our view of the earth's past. Steiner explains:

In that primeval time, the portion of the surface of the earth's globe today covered by the Atlantic Ocean was a mighty continent; while, where Europe, Asia and Africa are now situated scarcely any continents were formed. Thus it is that the solid matter, the very substance of the earth has been transformed as a result of its inner motion. For the planet earth is in a continual state of inner movement...[7]

W. Scott-Elliot (for whose work Steiner vouches, at least in externals) shows South America still separate as well as Atlantis, and the remains of a large older continent from the break-up of which the modern disposition of land-masses finally results.[8] Much of this makes good modern sense, once we understand how humanity retained a spiritual connection with these primal events. Since Steiner's day, science has come to the conclusion, already writ large in Steiner's evolutionary thought, that these processes follow large rhythmic patterns.[9] Behind the studies collected in this book stands that cosmic wisdom which reveals the connection of man with the whole evolution of the world. Steiner still has much to teach us, I believe, about the links between human evolution and these vast rhythms of creation—links which are to be discovered in the hidden structure of our consciousness itself.

Rudolf Steiner's writings and lectures on Atlantis, then, can open up exciting new vistas onto our own inner worlds, and, in their spiritual significance, onto the worlds that are only now being rediscovered by science in the primordial ages of humanity and our planet. I would only add one final note. Steiner makes rather frequent reference in some of these studies to the emergence of special characteristics among the different primitive races of mankind. He also reiterates on numerous occasions that this phase of racial differentiation belongs to the distant past. Nowadays all creative change of the kind we need comes from individuals, not from racial groupings, which have become irrelevant to humanity's modern form of existence. The title-page of Darwin's *Origin of Species* had contained a reference to 'natural selection' and to 'the preservation of favoured races'. Certain features of his thought plainly arose on the analogy of the competitive economics and empire-building of Victorian society. Or conversely, there were many who interpreted his evolutionary biology as implying that in the modern world too there would be 'dominant races' in the struggle for mastery over their environment. Rudolf Steiner rejected this approach in its entirety, and everywhere insisted that after prehistoric, Atlantean times in man's evolution one could speak only of developing cultures, cultural epochs, etc. This is a point he reiterates several times in the materials collected in this book. For him the concept of race belongs to the remoter past of humanity, and in modern times essentially has no reality. This aspect of his message needs to be emphasized even today, in our age which has learned a good deal about political correctness in such matters, but which retains a tendency to fall back all too easily on 'mass culture' and its stereotypes. These are further examples of tendencies that need to be overcome by spiritual thinking today. Rudolf Steiner's concept of the creatively evolving individual, able to discover the full potential within our ever-changing individual and cultural perspectives on reality, still beckons to us from the future.

1. The Continent of Atlantis

How is it possible to know what really happened in prehistory? Rudolf Steiner describes the inner connections which still exist in consciousness with the distant past, enabling even the remotest events to be 'remembered' by the initiates. He uncovers a world that is startling, yet makes profound sense today. Concepts such as the cyclic generation and movement of earth's land-masses contradicted the 'land-bridge' theories of his time, but now appear prophetic. Reaching far beyond the methods of ordinary history, Steiner opens the portals on a lost world that is nevertheless integral to the understanding of our own.

People can learn only a small part of what humanity experienced in prehistoric times through ordinary history. Historical documents shed light on no more than a few millennia. What archaeology, palaeontology and geology can teach us is very limited. Furthermore, everything built on external evidence is unreliable. One need only consider how the picture of an event or people not so very remote from us changes as new historical evidence is uncovered; one need only compare the descriptions of one and the same event by different historians to realize on what uncertain ground we stand in these matters. Everything belonging to the external world of the senses is subject to time. In addition, time destroys what has originated in time. On the other hand, external history is dependent on what has been preserved in time. We cannot say that the essential element has been preserved, if we remain content with the external evidence.

But everything which comes into being in time has its origin in the eternal, though the eternal is not accessible to sensory perception. Nevertheless, the ways to the perception of the eternal are open for human beings. They can develop forces dormant in them in order to recognize the eternal. This development is referred to in the book *How to Know the Higher Worlds*. These studies also show that at a certain high level of cognition, a person can penetrate to the eternal origins of those things which vanish with time. People have broadened their powers of cognition in this way when they are no longer limited to external evidence as far as knowledge of the past is concerned. Then they can see in events that part which is not perceptible to the senses, which time cannot destroy. They penetrate from transitory to non-transitory history.

It is a fact that this history is written in other characters than is ordinary history. In occult knowledge and theosophy it is called the 'Akashic Record'. Only a faint idea of this chronicle can be given in our language. For our language corresponds to the world of the senses. The things which are described by our language at once receive the character of this sense world. To the uninitiated, who cannot yet convince themselves of the reality of a separate spiritual world through their own experience, the initiate can easily appear to be a visionary, if not something worse.

People who have acquired the ability to perceive in the spiritual world come to know past events in their eternal character. Such events do not stand before them like the dead testimony of history, but appear in full life. It is almost as if what has happened takes place before them. Those initiated into the reading of such a living script can look back into a much more remote past than is represented by external history, and — on the basis of direct spiritual perception — they can also describe much more reliably the things of which history tells.

In order to avoid possible misunderstanding, it should be said that spiritual perception is not infallible. This perception also can err, can see in an inexact, oblique, wrong manner. No one is free from error in this field, no matter how high they stand. Therefore one should not complain when the communications of spiritual sources do not always entirely correspond. But the dependability of observation is much greater here than in the external world of the senses. What various initiates can relate about history and prehistory will essentially be in agreement. Such a history and prehistory does in fact exist in all Mystery schools. For millennia, agreement has been so complete here that the conformity existing among external historians of even a single century cannot be compared with it. The initiates describe essentially the same things at all times and in all places.

Several chapters from the Akashic Record will follow this introduction. First, those events will be described which took place when the so-called Atlantean continent still existed between America and Europe. This part of the earth's surface

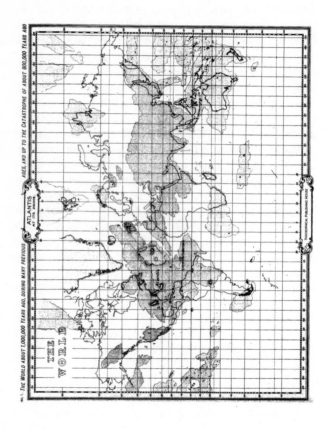

No. 1. THE WORLD ABOUT 1,000,000 YEARS AGO, DURING MANY PREVIOUS AGES, AND UP TO THE CATASTROPHE OF ABOUT 800,000 YEARS AGO

ATLANTIS AT ITS PRIME.

THE WORLD

THEOSOPHICAL PUBLISHING HOUSE

was once land. Today it forms the floor of the Atlantic ocean. Plato tells of the last remnant of this land, the island of Poseidonis, which lay westward of Europe and Africa.[10] *The Story of Atlantis and the Lost Lemuria* by W. Scott-Elliott describes how the floor of the Atlantic Ocean was once a continent, how for about a million years it was the scene of a civilization which, to be sure, was quite different from our modern ones, and the fact that the last remnants of this continent sank in the tenth millennium BC.[11] The present book is intended to provide information which will supplement Scott-Elliott's description. While he tends to describe the external events among our Atlantean ancestors, the aim here is to record some details concerning their spiritual character and the inner nature of the conditions under which they lived. Therefore the reader must go back in imagination to a period which lies almost ten thousand years in the past, and which lasted for many millennia. What is described here, however, did not take place only on the continent now covered by the waters of the Atlantic Ocean, but also in the neighbouring regions of what today is Asia, Africa, Europe

---

Opposite: Atlantis and the moving continents, as shown by Scott-Elliot; his work was affirmed as accurate at least in externals by Rudolf Steiner. Note how the Atlantean continent has not yet broken up to bring about the configuration of present North America, and South America has not yet moved across to join it. Asia and Australia are still joined in the remains of the archaic continent of 'Lemuria'. From W. Scott-Elliot, The Story of Atlantis *(1896).*

and America. What took place in these regions later developed from this earlier civilization.

The moving continents

We know that the earth is never at rest; we know that it is in a perpetual state of inner change and movement. It will be remembered from the description given of the Akashic Record, that the external aspect of the earth today is quite different from the aspect it presented, for example, at the time we call the Atlantean epoch. In this primeval epoch, the part of the surface of the earth which today is covered by the Atlantic Ocean was a mighty continent, while where Europe, Asia and Africa are now situated scarcely any continents were as yet formed. Thus the solid matter, the substance, of the earth has been transformed by its inner motion.

The planet earth is in a continual state of inner motion. Consider, for instance, that what we know today as the island of Heligoland is but a small part of that land which in the ninth and tenth centuries still projected out into the sea. The periods during which inner changes alter the earth's surface are comparatively great, yet even without going deeply into these matters we can see that our planet is in perpetual inner motion. Indeed, if we do not merely include the solid earth in the planet, but also the water and the air, then it is apparent in daily life that the planet is in inner motion. In the formation of clouds and rain, in all the phenomena of atmospheric conditions, in the rise and fall of the water, in all these we see the inner mobility of the planetary substance. That is a life process of the planet. Just as the etheric body works in the life of the individual, so do what we designate as the Spirits of Motion work in the life of the planet. We may therefore say: the external form of the planet is the creation of the Spirits of Form. The vitality is regulated by the beings we call the Spirits of Motion.[12]

2. The History of Atlantis

The idea of evolution as a 'trickle' of change producing humans out of animal ancestry has been extensively criticised and revised in modern times. Discoveries about our ancestors have shown that they were more human in some ways much earlier than was once assumed, yet lacked other features we take for granted in humanity until surprisingly late. Rudolf Steiner describes the quite different consciousness of early humanity, the different physical forms which they took, and the eventual emergence of thought in its first stages. Still a challenge to the evolutionary thought of today, the story of human origins he uncovers also offers many striking lessons on the ecological crisis of the contemporary world.

The earliest civilizations

Our Atlantean ancestors differed more from present-day man than anyone would imagine whose knowledge is confined wholly to the world of the senses. This difference extended not only to external appearance but also to spiritual faculties. Their knowledge, their technical skills, indeed their entire civilization differed from what can be observed today. If we go back to the first periods of Atlantean humanity we find a mental capacity quite different from ours. Logical reason, and the power of arithmetical combination, on which everything rests that is produced today, were totally absent among the first Atlanteans.

On the other hand, they had a highly developed memory. This memory was one of their most prominent mental faculties. For example, Atlanteans did not calculate as we do, by learning certain rules which they then applied. A 'multiplication table' was something totally unknown in Atlantean times. Nobody impressed upon their mind that three times four is twelve. In the event that they had to perform such a calculation, they could do so because they remembered identical or similar situations. They remembered how it had been on previous occasions. It has to be understood that each time a new faculty develops in an organism, an old faculty loses power and acuteness. People of today are superior to the Atlanteans in logical reasoning, in the ability to combine. On the other hand, memory has deteriorated. Nowadays people think in concepts; the Atlanteans thought in images. When an image appeared in their soul, they remembered a great many similar images which they had already experienced. They directed their judgement accordingly.

For this reason, all teaching at that time was different from what it became later. It was not calculated to furnish children with rules, to sharpen their reason. Instead, life was presented to them in vivid images, so that later they could remember as much as possible when they had to act under particular conditions. When the children had grown up and had gone out into life, they could remember something similar which had been presented to them in the course of their education for everything they had to do. They could manage best when the new situation was similar to one they had already seen. Under totally new conditions, the Atlantean had to rely on experiment. Much has been spared modern human beings in this respect due to the fact that they are equipped with rules which they can easily apply in any new situations. The Atlantean system of education gave a uniformity to all of life. Over long periods of time things were repeated as they had always been done. The Atlanteans' faithful memory did not allow anything to develop that was even remotely similar to the rapidity of progress as we experience it today. One did what one had always 'seen' before. One did not invent; one remembered. It was not the person who had learned much, but rather the person who had experienced much and therefore could remember much who was considered to be an authority. In the Atlantean period it would have been impossible for someone to decide an important matter before reaching a certain age. One had confidence only in a person who could look back upon long experience.

What has been said here was not true of the initiates and their schools. For they were in advance of the stage to which their age had developed. The decisive factor for admission into such schools was not age but whether in their previous incarnations applicants had acquired the faculties for receiving higher wisdom. The confidence placed in the initiates and their representatives during the Atlantean period was not based on the richness of their personal experience, but rather on the antiquity of their wisdom. With initiates, personality ceases to have any importance. They are totally in the service of eternal wisdom. Therefore the features which characterize a particular period do not apply to them.

While the power to think logically was absent among the Atlanteans (especially the earlier ones), they possessed something in their highly developed memory which gave a special character to everything they did. Other powers are always connected with the essential character of any given human power. Memory is more closely linked to the deeper foundation of man in nature than is reason, and in this context other powers were developed which were more closely connected to those of the subordinate beings of nature than are contemporary human powers. Thus the Atlanteans could control what we call the life force. In the same way that today we extract the energy of heat from coal and transform it into motive power for our means of transport, the Atlanteans knew how to put the germinal energy of organisms into the service of their technology. One can form an idea of this if we look at it in the following way. Think of seed grain. Energy lies dormant in it. This energy causes the stalk to sprout from the kernel. Nature can awaken this energy which reposes in the seed. Modern human beings cannot do it at will. They must bury the seed in the ground and leave its awakening to the forces of nature. Atlanteans could do something else. They knew how to change the energy of a pile of grain into technological power, just as modern human beings can change the heat energy of a pile of coal into such power. Plants were cultivated in the Atlantean period not merely for use as foodstuffs but also in order to make the energies dormant in them available to commerce and industry. Just as we have methods of transforming the energy dormant in coal into energy of motion in our steam engines, so the Atlanteans had devices which they fuelled — in a manner of speaking — with plant seeds, and in which the life force was transformed into technologically utilizable power. The vehicles of the Atlanteans, which floated a short distance above the ground, were moved in this way. These vehicles travelled at a height lower than that of the mountain ranges of the Atlantean period, and they had steering mechanisms by the aid of which they could rise above these mountain ranges.

One must imagine that with the passage of time all conditions on our earth have changed very much. Today, the above-mentioned vehicles of the Atlanteans would be totally useless. Their usefulness depended on the fact that at that time the cover of air which enveloped the earth was much denser than it is now. Whether in the face of current scientific beliefs one can easily imagine such greater density of air need not occupy us here. By their very nature, science and logical thinking can never decide what is possible or impossible. Their only function is to explain what has been ascertained by experience and observation. The above-mentioned density of air is as much a certainty for esoteric experience as any present-day fact given by the senses can be. Equally certain however is the fact, perhaps even more inexplicable for contemporary physics and chemistry, that at that time the water on the whole earth was much thinner than today. Because of this thinness the water could be directed by the germinal energy used by the Atlanteans into technical services which today are impossible. As a result of the increased density of water, it has become impossible to move and to direct it in such ingenious ways as once were possible.

From this it must be sufficiently clear that the civilization of the Atlantean period was radically different from ours. It will also be understood that the physical nature of an Atlantean was quite different from that of a contemporary person. An Atlantean took into himself water which could be used by the life force inherent in his own body in a manner quite different from what is possible in today's physical body. It was due to this that the Atlantean could consciously employ his physical powers in an entirely different way from a person today. He had, so to speak, the means to increase the physical powers in himself when he needed them for what he was doing. In order to have an accurate conception of the Atlanteans one must know that their ideas of fatigue and the depletion of forces were quite different from those of present-day man.

An Atlantean settlement — as must be evident from everything we have described — had a character which in no way resembled that of a modern city. In such a settlement everything was, on the contrary, still in alliance with nature. It is no more than a vaguely similar picture if we say that in the first Atlantean periods — about to the middle of the third sub-race — a settlement resembled a garden in which the houses were built of trees with artfully intertwined branches.

What the work of human hands created at that time grew out of nature. And people themselves felt wholly related to nature. Hence their social sense also was quite different from that of today. After all, nature is common to all human beings. What the Atlanteans built up on the basis of nature they considered to be common property just as people today think it only natural to consider as their private property what their ingenuity and intelligence have created for them. Anyone who familiarizes themselves with the idea that the Atlanteans were equipped with such spiritual and physical powers as have been described will also understand that in still earlier times mankind presented a picture which will remind them in only a few particulars of what they are accustomed to see today. Not only human beings, but also surrounding nature has changed enormously in the course of time. Plant and animal forms have become different. All of nature has been subjected to transformation. Once-inhabited regions of the earth have been destroyed; others have come into existence.

The ancestors of the Atlanteans lived in a region which has disappeared, the main part of which lay south of present-day Asia. In theosophical writings they are called the Lemurians. After they had passed through various stages of development, the greatest part of them declined. They became stunted and their descendants still inhabit certain parts of the earth today as so-called 'savage' tribes. But a small section of Lemurian humanity was capable of further development. From this part the Atlanteans were formed.

Later, something similar again took place. The greatest

part of the Atlantean population declined, and from a small portion the so-called Indo-Europeans descended who belong to present-day civilized humanity. According to the nomenclature of the science of the spirit, the Lemurians, Atlanteans and Indo-Europeans are root races of mankind. If one imagines that two such root races preceded the Lemurians and that two will succeed the Indo-Europeans in the future, one obtains a total seven. One always arises from the other in the manner just indicated with respect to the Lemurians, Atlanteans and Indo-Europeans. Each root race has physical and mental characteristics which are quite different from those of the preceding one.[13] While, for example, the Atlanteans especially developed memory and everything connected with it, at the present time it is the task of the Indo-Europeans to develop the faculty of thought and all that belongs to it.

Various stages must also be passed through in each root race. There are always seven of these. In the beginning of a period associated with a root race, its principal characteristics are in a youthful condition; slowly they attain maturity and finally enter a decline. The population of a root race is thus divided into seven sub-races. But one must not imagine that one sub-race immediately disappears when a new one develops. Each one may maintain itself for a long time while others are developing alongside it. Thus there are always populations which show different stages of development living together on earth.

The first sub-race of the Atlanteans developed from a very advanced part of the Lemurians who had a high evolutionary potential. The faculty of memory appeared only in its rudiments among the Lemurians, and then only in the last period of their development. We must imagine that while Lemurians could form ideas of what they were experiencing, they could not preserve these ideas. They immediately forgot what they had represented to themselves. But that they nevertheless lived in a certain civilization, that, for example, they had tools, erected buildings and so forth was owed not to their own powers of conception, but to a mental force within them which was, for want of a better word, instinctive. However, one must not imagine this to have been the present-day instinct of animals, but one of a different kind.

Theosophical writings call the first sub-race of the Atlanteans the Rmoahals. The memory of this race was primarily directed towards vivid sense impressions. Colours which the eye had seen, sounds which the ear had heard had a long after-effect in the soul. This was expressed in the fact that the Rmoahals developed feelings which their Lemurian ancestors did not yet know. For example, the attachment to past experience was a part of these feelings.

The development of memory was connected with that of language. As long as human beings did not preserve the past, there could be no communication through the medium of language of what had been experienced. The appearance of first beginnings of memory in the final Lemurian period meant that it was also possible for the faculty of giving a name to what had been seen and heard to have its inception. Only human beings who have the faculty of recollection can make use of a name which has been given to something. The Atlantean period, therefore, is the one in which the development of language took place. With language, a bond was established between the human soul and the things outside the human being. People produced sound-words inside themselves and these sound-words belonged to the objects of the external world. A new bond is formed also among human beings by communication through the medium of language. It is true that all this existed in a still youthful form among the Rmoahals, but nevertheless it distinguished them profoundly from their Lemurian forefathers.

The soul powers of these first Atlanteans still possessed something of the forces of nature. These people were more closely related to the beings of nature which surrounded them than were their successors. Their soul powers were more connected with forces of nature than are those of modern human beings. Thus the sound-word which they produced had something of the power of nature. They not only named things, but their words contained a power over things and also over their fellow human beings. The word of the Rmoahals not only had meaning, but also power. The magic power of words is something which was far truer for them than it is for people today. When a Rmoahals person pronounced a word, this word developed a power similar to that of the object it designated. Because of this, words at that time were curative; they could advance the growth of plants, tame the rage of animals and perform other similar functions. All this progressively decreased in force among the later sub-races of the Atlanteans. One could say that the original fullness of power was gradually lost.

The Rmoahals felt this plenitude of power to be a gift of mighty nature, and their relationship to the latter had a religious character. For them language was something especially sacred. The misuse of certain sounds, which possessed an important power, was an impossibility. They felt that such misuse would cause them enormous harm. The good magic of such words would have changed into its opposite; something that would have brought blessing if used properly would bring ruin to the author if used criminally. In a kind of innocence of feeling, the Rmoahals ascribed their power not so much to themselves as to divine nature acting within them.

This changed among the second sub-race, the so-called Tlavatli peoples. The people of this race began to develop a sense of their own personal value. Ambition, a quality unknown to the Rmoahals, made itself felt among them. Memory in a certain sense became part of their conception of the nature of communal life. A person who could look back upon certain deeds he had performed demanded recognition of them from his fellow human beings. Such a person would demand that his works be preserved in memory. Based upon this memory of deeds, groups of people belonging together would elect one person from amongst themselves as leader. A kind of royal rank developed. Such recognition was even preserved beyond death. The memory, the remembrance of the ancestors or of those who had acquired merit in life, developed. From this there emerged among some tribes a

kind of religious veneration of the deceased, a cult of
ancestor worship. This cult continued into much later times
and took the most varied forms. Among the Rmoahals it was
still the case that a person was esteemed only to the degree to
which he commanded respect at a given moment through his
powers. If someone among them wanted recognition for
what he had done in earlier days, he had to demonstrate by
new deeds that he still possessed his old power. He had to
recall the old works to memory by means of new ones. What
had been done was not recognized for its own sake. Only the
second sub-race considered the personal character of a person to the point where it took his past life into account in the
evaluation of his character.

A further consequence of memory for the communal life of
human beings was the fact that groups were formed which
were held together by the remembrance of common deeds.
Previously, the formation of groups depended wholly upon
natural forces, upon common descent. Human beings did
not add anything through their own mind to what nature
had made of them. Now a powerful personality would
recruit a number of people for a joint undertaking, and the
memory of this joint action formed a social group.

This kind of social communal life became fully developed
only among the third sub-race, the Toltecs. It was therefore
the people of this race who first founded what can be called a
community, the first method of forming a state. The leadership, the government of these communities, was transmitted
from one generation to the next. The father now passed on to
the son what previously survived only in the memory of

contemporaries. The deeds of the ancestors were not to be forgotten by their whole line of descent. What an ancestor had done was honoured in his descendants. However, one must realize that in those times people actually had the power to transmit their gifts to their descendants. Education, after all, was calculated to mould life through vivid images. The effectiveness of this education had its foundation in the personal power which emanated from the educator. He did not sharpen the power of thought, but developed those gifts which were of a more instinctive kind. Through such a system of education the capacities of the father were in most cases transmitted to the son.

Under such circumstances personal experience acquired more and more importance among the third sub-race. When one group of human beings separated from another, it took along for the foundation of a new community the remembrance of what it had experienced at the place of its previous existence. But at the same time there was something in this memory which the group did not find suitable for itself, with which it did not feel at ease. Therefore it then tried something new. Thus conditions improved every time that such a new community was established. It was only natural that what was better should be imitated. These are the facts which explain the development of the flourishing communities in the period of the third sub-race, described in theosophical literature. These acquired personal experiences were supported by those who were initiated into the eternal laws of spiritual development. Powerful rulers themselves were initiated, so that personal ability might have full support. Through their personal abilities, human beings slowly prepared themselves for initiation. They first had to develop their powers from the bottom up in order that enlightenment from above could be given to them. In this way the initiated kings and leaders of the Atlanteans were created. Enormous power lay in their hands, and they were greatly venerated.

But this circumstance also contained the cause for decline and decay. The development of memory led to the pre-eminent power of personality. Human beings wanted to count for something through their power. The greater their power became, the more they wanted to exploit it for themselves. The ambition which had developed turned into manifest selfishness. Thus the misuse of these powers arose. When one considers the capabilities of the Atlanteans resulting from their mastery of the life force, one will understand that such misuse inevitably had enormous consequences. Wide-ranging power over nature could be put at the service of personal egotism. This was accomplished in full measure by the fourth sub-race, the First Turanians. The members of this race, who were instructed in the mastery of the powers described above, often used them in order to satisfy their selfish wishes and desires. But used in such a manner, these powers destroy each other in their reciprocal effects. It is as if the feet were stubbornly to carry a man forward while his torso wanted to go backward.

Such a destructive effect could only be halted through the development of a higher faculty in human beings. This was the faculty of thought. Logical thinking has a restraining effect on selfish personal desires.

The beginnings of thought

The origin of logical thinking must be sought among the fifth sub-race, the Original Semites. Human beings began to go beyond a mere remembrance of the past and to compare different experiences. The faculty of judgement developed. Wishes and appetites were regulated in accordance with this faculty of judgment. People began to calculate, to combine. People learned to work with thoughts. If previously people had abandoned themselves to every desire, now they first asked whether their thinking could approve this desire. While the people of the fourth sub-race rushed wildly towards the satisfaction of their desires, those of the fifth began to listen to an inner voice. This inner voice restrains the desires, although it cannot destroy the claims of the selfish personality.

Thus the fifth sub-race transferred the impulses for action to within the human being. Human beings wished to come to terms within themselves as to what they should or should not do. But the benefit which accrued inwardly with respect to the faculty of thought was lost with respect to the control of external natural forces. For such combinatorial thinking can master only the forces of the mineral world, not the life force. The fifth sub-race therefore developed thought at the expense of control of the life force. But it was precisely in this way that it produced the germ which would allow the onward development of humankind. Now personality, self-love, even complete selfishness could grow freely; for thought alone, which works wholly within and can no longer give direct orders to nature, is not capable of producing such devastating effects as the previously misused powers. From this fifth sub-race the most gifted part was selected which survived the decline of the fourth root race and formed the germ of the fifth, the Indo-European peoples, whose mission is the complete development of the faculty of thinking.

The people of the sixth sub-race, the Akkadians, developed the faculty of thought even further than the fifth. They differed from the so-called Original Semites in that they employed this faculty in a more comprehensive sense than the former.

It has been said that while the development of the faculty of thought prevented the claims of the selfish personality from having the same devastating effects as among the earlier races, these claims were not destroyed by it. The Original Semites at first arranged their personal circumstances as their faculty of thought directed. Intelligence took the place of mere appetites and desires. The conditions of life changed. If preceding races were inclined to acknowledge as leader one whose deeds had impressed themselves deeply upon their memory, or who could look back upon a life of rich memories, this role was now conferred upon the intelligent.

If previously that which lived in clear remembrance was decisive, one now regarded as best what was most convincing in thought. Under the influence of memory, one

formerly held fast to a thing until it was found to be inade-
quate, and in such a case it was quite natural that the person
who was in a position to remedy a want could introduce an
innovation. But as a result of the faculty of thought, a fond-
ness for innovations and changes developed. Each person
wanted to put into effect what his intelligence suggested to
him. Turbulent conditions therefore began to prevail under
the fifth sub-race, and in the sixth this led to a feeling that the
obdurate thinking of the individual needed to be made
subject to general laws. The splendour of the communities of
the third sub-race was based on the fact that common
memories brought about order and harmony. In the sixth,
this order had to be brought about by thought-out laws. Thus
it is in this sixth sub-race that one must look for the origin of
the regulation of justice and law.

During the third sub-race, the separation of a group took
place only when it was forced out of its community, so to
speak, because it no longer felt at ease in the conditions
prevailing as a result of memory. In the sixth this was con-
siderably different. The calculating faculty of thinking
sought the new as such; it promoted enterprises and the
establishment of something new. The Akkadians were
therefore an enterprising people with an inclination to
colonization. It was commerce, especially, which nourished
the waxing faculty of thought and judgement.

Among the seventh sub-race, the Mongols, the faculty of
thought also developed. But characteristics of the earlier sub-
races, especially of the fourth, remained present in them to a
much higher degree than in the fifth and sixth. They

remained faithful to the feeling for memory. And thus they reached the conclusion that what is oldest is also what is most sensible and can best defend itself against the faculty of thought. It is true that they lost the mastery over the life forces, but what developed in them as the faculty of thinking nevertheless possessed something of the natural might of this life force. Indeed, they had lost the power over life, but they never lost their direct, naive faith in it. This force had become their god, on whose behalf they did everything they considered right. Thus they appeared to neighbouring peoples as if possessed by this secret force, and they surrendered themselves to it in blind trust. Their descendants in Asia and in some parts of Europe manifested and still manifest much of this quality.

The faculty of thought planted in human beings could only attain its full value in relation to human development when it received a new impetus in the fifth root race. The fourth root race, after all, could only put this faculty at the service of that to which it was educated through the gift of memory. The fifth alone reached life conditions for which the proper tool is the ability to think.

3. Etheric Technology: Atlantean 'Magic' Powers

As we re-examine our modern sources of energy, based on the exploitation of nature, Rudolf Steiner shows us the quite different ways in which early humanity was able to manipulate forces 'magically', i.e. by a connection from within, by fusing one's consciousness together with nature rather than standing back to control it from outside. Our consciousness has changed enormously over millennia of evolution — yet it is Steiner's contention that such forces can once again fall under human spiritual control.

Etheric technology

During the whole first half of Atlantis, the texture of the human body was much softer, much more flexible, and yielded to the forces of the soul. These soul forces were essentially more powerful than they are today, and they both shaped and overpowered the physical body. A person in ancient Atlantis would have been able to break a section of rail from a railway, let us say, with ease — not because his physical forces were strong, for his bony system had still not developed, but through his magical, psychic forces. A cannon ball, for example, could have been repulsed by this psychic force. The density of flesh developed only later. A similar phenomenon is still to be found today in certain pathological cases who on account of the liberation of strong psychic forces — in that condition the physical body is not properly connected with the higher bodies — can lift and throw heavy objects.

Because in Atlantis a person's physical body was still pliable, such a person could more easily adjust to processes in the life of the soul; physical stature could be made to decrease or increase in size. If, for example, a person in Atlantis was, let us say, stupid or sensual he fell into matter, as it were, and became a giant in stature. The more intelligent human beings developed a delicate constitution and were smaller in stature; those who were dull-witted were giants. A person's external form was influenced to a far greater extent by the forces of the soul than is the case today when matter has become inflexible. The bodies of people developed in accordance with their qualities of soul and this accounted for the great differences in the races.

If the evolution of humanity until the middle of the Atlantean epoch had proceeded without the influence of Lucifer,[14] human beings would by then have developed a picture consciousness imbued with a high degree of clairvoyance. There would have been in their souls something that through its power would have revealed the external world to them in inner pictures; they would not have perceived objects outside through their eyes. As a result of the luciferic influence, human beings perceived the physical world at an early stage, but they did not do so in the right way. They saw the external world as if through a veil. The divine spiritual beings had planned evolution for them in

such a way that in place of the dull, clairvoyant consciousness with which their inner world was perceived in pictures,
they would so have perceived the external world that the
spirit would have been present behind everything material.
They would have seen the spirit behind the physical world.

All of a sudden—please do not take this literally, for the
process would obviously have taken some time—the external world would, without Lucifer, have appeared to human
beings at a given time; they would have awakened. The inner
world would have suddenly vanished, but the consciousness
of the spirit in which that world originated would have
remained. Human beings would have seen not only the
plants, animals and so forth but simultaneously the spirit
from which they had come forth. But because the luciferic
beings drew human beings down to the earth too soon, the
external world had the effect of hiding the world of spirit
from them. Physical matter became opaque for them.
Otherwise, they would have seen through it to the primordial spiritual ground of the world. Because human
beings had come down too soon into matter, it proved to be
too dense for them and they could not penetrate it. But from
the middle of the Atlantean epoch onward, other retarded
spiritual beings were able to penetrate this matter, in consequence of which it became clouded and human beings
were no longer able to behold the spiritual. These were the
ahrimanic or Mephistophelian beings.

Mephistopheles or Ahriman is not the same being as
Lucifer. Through untruth—Zarathustra calls Ahriman the
Lie—he clouds the purity of spirit of human beings, conceals

the spirit from them. Ahriman follows Lucifer and instils into human beings the illusion that matter is a reality in itself. So in the course of their evolution, during which the divine-spiritual beings wanted their influence to work upon them, human beings allowed themselves to be subject to two other influences: those of Lucifer who attacks human beings in their inner nature, in their astral body, endeavouring to confuse and mislead them; and Ahriman who, working from outside, deludes human beings to a certain extent, causing the external world to appear as *maya*, as matter. Lucifer is the spirit who is active within human beings. Ahriman, in contrast, is the spirit who spreads matter like a veil over the spiritual and makes recognition of the spiritual world impossible. These two spirits hold human beings back in the development of their spirituality. It was especially the ahrimanic influence that asserted itself in human beings and caused the Atlantean part of the earth to perish.

In Lemuria, human beings had a strong effect upon nature with their magical forces. They could, for example, control fire. The Atlanteans were no longer capable of this. But with their will they could control the germinal forces in which deep secrets lie hidden—the forces of air and water. Fire was beyond their control. Let us be clear that when we look at a locomotive today, constructed and controlled by human beings, this is something quite different. Today human beings understand how to make the forces contained in coal serve their purposes, to turn them into a propelling power. This process means that they control the lifeless, mineral force in the coal. The Atlanteans, however, controlled the actual life force contained in seeds. Think of the life force that causes the blades of grass to sprout from the earth. This life force was extracted from the seed by the Atlanteans and put to use. In their sheds where the Atlanteans kept their 'air ships', they laid up enormous stocks of seeds, just as we today store coal. They propelled their vehicles with the power accumulated from the seeds. When the clairvoyant looks back to that age, he sees these vehicles near the earth in the air that was still denser; equipped with a kind of control mechanism, they rose up and moved. The Atlanteans controlled these forces. Now it is unthinkable to imagine that the forces of plants — soul forces, that is to say — can be applied by magical means without at the same time influencing the forces of air and water. When the will of the Atlanteans turned to evil and used these forces for egotistical purposes, they simultaneously evoked the forces of water and of air, released them, and ancient Atlantis perished as a result. The continents came into existence through the cooperation of the elements and human beings. At the same time the ahrimanic influence was gradually able to become so strong that human beings could no longer see the spiritual. Behind physical matter they could see nothing except the mineral, inorganic element, and that meant that the magical powers vanished ever more completely from them.

In the Atlantean epoch, human beings were able to control and master the life force in the plant kingdom. In the Lemurian age it lay within their power to control the seminal forces of animals, and indeed it actually came to the point of Lemurian people applying these seminal forces of animals to transform animal forms into human forms. Every such magical action performed by human beings with these seminal forces causes a release of the forces of fire. When such will becomes evil, the worst forces of black magic are generated and evoked. Today the most evil forces on the earth are still released when black magicians mishandle forces that are, generally speaking, withheld from mankind. These forces are powerful and at the same time holy. They are forces that, in the wise hands of worthy guides, can be applied in the highest and purest service of humanity.

Human beings now gradually became incapable of moulding their bodies. Cartilage and bones, the hard constituents, were integrated into them and the resemblance of human beings to their present shape constantly increased. It was in the Atlantean epoch that this first took place and it is therefore comprehensible that ancient Atlantis cannot be found by modern researchers. Hopes cherished by academics of still being able to find traces of human evolution in these ancient times will never be fulfilled, because human beings were then beings whose limbs still consisted of soft, flabby substance. Such a body cannot be preserved, just as after a hundred years no remnants of the soft-bodied molluscs are to be found. Remnants of animals from ancient periods can still be found because the animals had already hardened while the human constitution was still soft and pliable. The animals came down into matter too soon; they were not able to wait. Out of the earliest human figures, who had become physical too soon, the most stunted human figures came into existence. The noblest human figures stayed above the earth the longest, and remained soft and pliable. They waited until they were able to avoid an age during which they would have been obliged to remain stationary at a certain stage of hardening, as in the case of the animals. Because they were not able to wait, the animals have remained at a stage of rigidity and hardening.

The evolution of the earth has now been described up to the time when the forces of water were unleashed and ancient Atlantis perished. The human beings who were saved from Atlantis made their way in the one direction towards America and in the other towards the Europe, Asia and Africa of today. These great migrations continued over long periods of time.

Let us now consider ancient Atlantean culture once more. In the earliest period man possessed strong magical powers. With these powers he controlled the seed forces, mastered the forces of nature and in a certain way was still able to see into the spiritual world. Clairvoyance then gradually faded because human beings were destined to found the culture belonging to the earth; they were to descend to earth in the real sense. Thus at the end of Atlantis there were two kinds of human beings within the peoples and races. Firstly, at the height of Atlantean culture there were seers, clairvoyants and powerful magicians who worked by means of magical forces and were able to see into the spiritual world. Besides them were people who were preparing to be the founders of present humanity. They already had within them the rudiments of the faculties possessed by people today.

They were no longer able to equal the achievements of the

old Atlanteans in any way but they were able to make pre-paration for intelligence, for the power of judgement. They possessed the elementary faculties of calculation, counting, combination and so forth. They were the people who developed the rudiments of the intelligence of today and no longer made use of the magical forces applied by the Atlantean magicians at the time when their application was already fraught with danger on account of the powerful ahrimanic influences. They were the 'others', the despised people, rather like the anthroposophists today who meet together in small groups, or like the first Christians in ancient Rome who gathered together in the catacombs.

Twilight of the magicians

Now in Atlantis there were also centres of culture and ritual — we will call them the Atlantean Oracles — where what is called Atlantean wisdom was harboured and prac-tised. The great leader of the Sun Oracle, the greatest initiate of Atlantis, directed his attention above all to that section of human beings who differed from the ordinary population in ancient Atlantis. They were simple people who were looked down upon and who no longer possessed magical powers. But it was they who were gathered together by the great initiate because they had developed the new faculties, even if only in a primitive form. It was from them that under-standing of the new age was to be expected. The great initiate gathered together this useful material for the future, and also those old initiates or magicians who had not persisted in clinging egotistically to the former practices. Our present age presents a similar picture and can be compared with the conditions prevailing in Atlantis at that time. Today, too, there are on the one side influential figures in the prevailing forms of culture, people who in their own way are magicians, working only with what is inorganic; on the other side, there are the despised people who even today want to work for the future. At that time, in Atlantis, the members of that culture, the old magicians, also looked down disparagingly upon the small number of those who had developed the new faculty, which was useless in ancient Atlantis.

The great initiate of the Sun Oracle did not, however, despise these people. Today, too, the proud bearers of our culture look down upon a small number of human beings, upon the anthroposophists who gather in small, insignificant meeting places and are said to engage in all kinds of foolish activities. Generally speaking, they are unprofessional laymen who claim to be inaugurating the future. These are the people who are developing and preparing in themselves a faculty that to the others seems useless, but because it carries a hint of the future it is able to create a connection again with the spiritual world. In Atlantis long ago it was a matter of finding the connection with the physical, material world; the task today is to discover the spiritual again. Just as at that time the old initiate gathered his host together locally, directing his call to the simple, despised people, so today again, under different—not local—conditions, a call goes forth from the great Masters of Wisdom who are allowing certain spiritual treasures of wisdom to flow into humanity. Those possessed of certain qualities respond to this call as did certain human beings long ago; they were individuals who had within them primitive talents for calculation, computation and so forth.

This wisdom is not imparted simply for anthroposophical dogmas to be grasped by the intellect but to understand them with the heart. One is then strong enough to know why anthroposophy is here today. It is here to meet a great challenge of evolution, and the person who knows this also finds the strength to conquer all obstacles, come what may. Such people proceed along their path because they know that what is intended to come to pass through anthroposophy must come to pass for the further progress of humanity on the path to the spirit.

The great initiate of the Sun Oracle led the small group of human beings and founded a kind of cultural centre in Asia. He drew these individuals to him in order to make them capable of founding post-Atlantean culture. During the great migration, everything that had come into existence in Atlantis had been mingled, jumbled together. It follows that in the post-Atlantean epoch one should no longer speak of races but of civilizations, cultures.

4. The Divine Messengers

We have seen in outline how, almost from the beginning of human history, the guidance and development of humanity was entrusted to the initiates, the 'divine messengers'. Never was their power and influence greater than in the times of ancient Atlantis. But as they developed the human qualities of independent thought and self-will, the scene was at the same time being set for one of the greatest disasters ever to befall humanity, spiritually and physically. The one who had the mission of uniting the best of all these qualities for the future of mankind was the figure known to legend as Manu.

What has previously been said about the fourth root race, the Atlanteans, refers to the great bulk of mankind. But they followed leaders whose abilities towered far above theirs. The wisdom these leaders possessed and the powers at their command were not to be attained by any earthly education. They had been imparted to them by higher beings which did not belong directly to earth. Therefore it was only natural that the great mass of people felt their leaders to be beings of a higher kind, to be 'messengers' of the gods. For what these leaders knew and could do would not have been attainable by human sense organs and by human reason. They were venerated as 'divine messengers' and people accepted their orders, their commandments, and also their instruction. It was by beings of this kind that mankind was instructed in the sciences, in the arts, and in the making of tools. Such 'divine messengers' either directed the communities themselves or instructed human beings who were sufficiently advanced in the art of government. It was said of these leaders that they 'communicate with the gods' and were initiated by the gods themselves into the laws according to which humankind had to develop. This was true. In places about which the average person knew nothing, this initiation, this communication with the gods, actually took place. These places of initiation were called temples of the Mysteries. From them the human race was directed.

What took place in the temples of the mysteries was therefore incomprehensible to the people. Equally little did the latter understand the intentions of their great leaders. After all, the people could grasp with their senses only what happened directly upon the earth, not what was revealed from higher worlds for the welfare of the earth. Therefore the teachings of the leaders had to be expressed in a form unlike communications about earthly events. The language the gods spoke with their messengers in the Mysteries was not earthly, and neither were the shapes in which these gods revealed themselves. The higher spirits appeared to their messengers 'in fiery clouds' in order to tell them how they were to lead human beings. Only human beings can appear in human form; entities whose capacities tower above the human must reveal themselves in shapes which are not to be found on earth.

Because they themselves were the most perfect among

their fellow human beings, the 'divine messengers' could receive these revelations. They had already gone through in earlier stages what the majority of human beings still had to experience. They belonged among their fellow humans only in a certain respect. They could assume human form. But their spiritual-mental qualities were of a superhuman kind. Thus they were divine-human hybrid beings. One can also describe them as higher spirits who assumed human bodies in order to help humankind forward on its earthly path. The real home of these beings was not on earth.

These divine-human beings led people without being able to inform them of the principles by which they directed them. For until the fifth sub-race of the Atlanteans, the Original Semites, human beings had absolutely no capacities for understanding these principles. The faculty of thought, which developed in this sub-race, was such a capacity. But this evolved slowly and gradually. Even the last sub-races of the Atlanteans could understand very little of the principles of their divine leaders. They began, at first quite imperfectly, to have a presentiment of such principles. Therefore their thoughts and also the laws which we have mentioned in the context of their governmental institutions were divined at rather than clearly thought out.

The principal leader of the fifth Atlantean sub-race gradually prepared it so that in later times, after the decline of the Atlantean way of life, it could begin a new one which was to be wholly directed by the faculty of thought.

One must realize that at the end of the Atlantean period there existed three groups of human-like beings. First, there were the above-mentioned 'divine messengers' who in their development were far ahead of the great mass of the people, and who taught divine wisdom and accomplished divine deeds. Second, there was the great mass of humanity, among which the faculty of thought was in a dull condition, although they possessed natural abilities which modern human beings have lost. Third was a small group of those who were developing the faculty of thought. While they gradually lost the natural abilities of the Atlanteans through this process, they were advancing to the stage where they could grasp the principles of the 'divine messengers' with their thoughts.

The second group of human beings was doomed to gradual extinction. The third, however, could be trained by a being of the first kind to take its direction into its own hands.

From this third group, the principal leader mentioned above, whom esoteric literature refers to as Manu, selected the ablest in order that a new humanity could emerge from them. These most capable ones existed in the fifth sub-race. The faculty of thought of the sixth and seventh sub-races had already gone astray in a certain sense and was no longer suitable for further development. The best qualities of the best people had to be developed. This was accomplished by the leader through the isolation of the selected group in a certain place on earth—in Central Asia—where they were freed from any influence of those who remained behind or of those who had gone astray.

The task which the leader imposed upon himself was to bring his followers to the point where, in their own soul, with their own faculty of thought, they could grasp the principles according to which they had hitherto been directed in a way vaguely sensed, but not clearly recognized. Human beings were to recognize the divine forces which they had unconsciously followed. Up to that point the gods had led human beings through their messengers; now they were to acquire knowledge about these divine entities. They were to learn to consider themselves as the implementing organs of divine providence.

The isolated group thus faced an important decision. The divine leader was in their midst, in human form. From such divine messengers human beings had previously received instructions and orders as to what they were or were not to do. Human beings had been instructed in the sciences which dealt with what they could perceive through the senses. Human beings had vaguely sensed a divine control of the world, had felt it in their own actions, but they had not known anything of it clearly.

Now their leader spoke to them in a completely new way. He taught them that invisible powers directed what confronted them visibly, and that they themselves were servants of these invisible powers, that they had to fulfil the laws of these invisible powers with their thoughts. Human beings were told of the supernatural and divine. They heard that the invisible spiritual element was the creator and preserver of the visible physical element. Up to that point they had looked up to their visible divine messengers, to the superhuman initiates, and through the latter was communicated what was and was not to be done. But now they were considered worthy of having the divine messenger speak to them of the gods themselves. Mighty were the words which again and again he impressed upon his followers: 'Until now you have seen those who led you; but there are higher leaders whom you do not see. It is these leaders to whom you are subject. You shall carry out the orders of the God whom you do not see; and you shall obey one of whom you can make no image for yourselves.' Thus did the new and highest commandment come from the mouth of the great leader, prescribing the veneration of a god whom no sensory-visible image could resemble and of whom none was therefore to be made. The well-known commandment which follows is an echo of this great fundamental commandment of the fifth human root race: 'Thou shalt not make unto thee any graven image, or any likeness of any thing that is in heaven above, or that is in the earth beneath, or that is in the water under the earth' (Exodus 20:31).

The principal leader, Manu, was assisted by other divine messengers who executed his intentions with regard to particular areas of life and worked on the development of the new race. For it was a matter of arranging all of life according to the new conception of a divine administration of the world. Everywhere the thoughts of human beings were to be directed from the visible to the invisible. Life is determined by the forces of nature. The course of human life depends on day and night, on winter and summer, on sunshine and rain. How these influential visible events are connected with the invisible, divine powers and how human beings were to behave in order to arrange their life in accordance with these invisible powers was shown to them. All knowledge and all labour was to be pursued in this sense. In the course of the stars and of the weather, man was to see divine decrees, the emanation of divine wisdom. Astronomy and meteorology were taught with this idea. Man was to arrange his labour, his moral life in such a way that they would correspond to the wise laws of the divine. Life was ordered according to divine commandments, just as the divine thoughts were explored in the course of the stars and in the changes of the weather. Man was to bring his works into harmony with the dispensations of the gods through sacrificial acts.

It was the intention of Manu to direct everything in human life towards the higher worlds. All human activities, all institutions were to bear a religious character.[15] By this means Manu wanted to initiate the real task imposed upon the fifth root race. This race was to learn to direct itself by its own thoughts. But such self-determination can only lead to good if human beings also place themselves at the service of the higher powers. Human beings should use their faculty of thought, but this faculty of thought should be sanctified by being devoted to the divine.

One can only understand completely what happened at that time if one knows that the development of the faculty of thought, beginning with the fifth sub-race of the Atlanteans, also entailed something else. From a certain quarter, human beings had come into possession of knowledge and of arts which were not immediately connected with what Manu had to consider as his true task. This knowledge and these arts were at first devoid of religious character. They came to human beings in such a way that they could think of nothing other than to place them at the service of self-interest, of their personal needs.[16] Such knowledge, for example, included the use of fire for human activities.

In early Atlantean times human beings did not use fire since the life force was available for them to use. But with the passage of time they were less and less in a position to make use of this force, hence they had to learn to make tools, utensils from so-called lifeless objects. They employed fire for this purpose. Similar conditions prevailed with respect to other natural forces. Thus human beings learned to make use of such natural forces without being conscious of their divine origin. So it was meant to be. Human beings were not to be forced by anything to relate these things which served their faculty of thought to the divine order of the world. They were, rather, to do it voluntarily in their thoughts. It was the intention of Manu to bring human beings to the point where, independently, out of an inner need, they brought such things into a relation with the higher order of the world. Human beings could choose whether they wanted to use the insight they had attained purely in a spirit of personal self-interest or in the religious service of a higher world.

If human beings were previously forced to consider themselves as a link in the divine government of the world, by which, for example, the domination over the life force was given to them without having to use the faculty of thought, they could now employ the natural forces without directing their thoughts to the divine.

Not all the human beings whom Manu had gathered

around him were equal to this decision; indeed, only a few of them were. It was from these few that Manu could really form the seeds of the new race. He withdrew with them in order to further their development while the others mingled with the rest of mankind.

From this small number of human beings who finally gathered around Manu, everything is descended which, up to the present, forms the true seeds of progress of the fifth root race. For this reason also, two characteristics run through the entire development of this fifth root race. One of these characteristics is peculiar to those who are animated by higher ideas, who regard themselves as children of a divine universal power; the other belongs to those who put everything at the service of personal interests, of egotism.

The small group of followers remained gathered around Manu until it had gathered sufficient strength to act in the new spirit, and until its members could go out to bring this new spirit to the rest of mankind which remained from the earlier races. It is natural that this new spirit assumed a different character among the various peoples, according to how they themselves had developed in different fields. The old remaining characteristics blended with what the messengers of Manu carried to the various parts of the world. Thus a variety of new cultures and civilizations came into being.

The ablest personalities from the circle around Manu were selected for a gradual direct initiation into his divine wisdom, so that they could become the teachers of the others. A new kind of initiate thus was added to the old divine messengers. It consisted of those who had developed their faculty of thought in an earthly manner just as their fellow human beings had done. The earlier divine messengers — and also Manu — had not done this. Their development belonged to higher worlds. They introduced their higher wisdom to earthly conditions. What they gave to mankind was a 'gift from above'. Before the middle of the Atlantean period, human beings had not reached the point where by their own powers they could grasp what the divine decrees were. Now — at the time indicated — they were to attain this point. Earthly thinking was to elevate itself to the concept of the divine. The human initiates united themselves with the divine. This represents an important revolution in the development of the human race.

The first Atlanteans did not as yet have a choice as to whether or not they would consider their leaders to be divine messengers. For what the latter accomplished imposed itself as the deed of higher worlds. It bore the stamp of divine origin. Thus the messengers of the Atlantean period were entities sanctified by their power, surrounded by the splendour which this power conferred upon them. From an external point of view, the human initiates of later times were human beings among human beings. But they remained in contact with the higher worlds and the revelations and manifestations of the divine messengers came to them. Only in exceptional circumstances, when a higher necessity arose, did they make use of certain powers which were conferred upon them from above. Then they accomplished deeds which human beings could not explain by the laws they know and which therefore they rightly regarded as miracles.

But in all this the higher intention is to make mankind stand on its own two feet, fully to develop its faculty of thought. Today the human initiates are the mediators between the people and the higher powers, and only initiation can make one capable of communication with the divine messengers.

The human initiates, the sacred teachers, became leaders of the rest of mankind in the beginning of the fifth root race. The great prehistoric priest kings, of whom legend rather than history tells, belong to these initiates. The higher divine messengers increasingly retired from the earth and left the leadership to these human initiates whom, however, they assisted in word and deed. Were this not so, human beings would never attain free use of their faculty of thought. The world is under divine direction, but human beings are not to be forced to admit it; they are to realize and to understand it by free reflection. When they reach this point, the initiates will gradually divulge their secrets to them. But this cannot happen all at once. The whole development of the fifth root race is a slow road to this goal. At first Manu himself led his following like children. Then leadership was gradually transferred to the human initiates. Today progress still consists in a mixture of conscious and unconscious acting and thinking of human beings. Only at the end of the fifth root race, when throughout the sixth and seventh sub-races a sufficiently great number of human beings have become capable of knowledge, will the greatest among the initiates be able to reveal himself to them openly. Then this human initiate will be able to assume the principal leadership just as Manu did at the end of the fourth root race. Thus the education of the fifth root race consists in this, that a greater part of humanity will become able freely to follow a human Manu in the same way that the germinal race of this fifth root race followed the divine one.

5. Atlantean Secret Knowledge: Its Betrayal and Subsequent Fate

Rudolf Steiner widens the perspective dramatically to reveal the cosmic dimension of the struggle that was emerging in the development of humanity. Not only the future of human beings but the balance of cosmic forces affecting the whole earth — and even beyond — was at stake. In describing the events leading to terrible catastrophe, Steiner also reveals how Manu was the representative of the Sun-power in spiritual evolution, that is, of the redeeming power we know as the Christ. As a Christ-initiate long before the earthly appearance of Christ, he was therefore able to bring to bear on human evolution the spiritual forces that would give to man moral individuality. Hence, although the secret knowledge of Atlantis was lost through the betrayal of the Oracles, there would come a time when through Christianity human beings would be able to be in equilibrium once again with the divine-cosmic powers.

During the Atlantean age, it was possible for some individuals to be entangled in the world of the senses to a minimal extent. This transformed the luciferic influence from an obstacle to human evolution into an instrument of further progress that put these individuals in a position to develop their knowledge of earthly things earlier than would have been possible otherwise. As part of this process, these people attempted to eliminate error from their mental activity and to discover the original intentions of spiritual beings in the phenomena of the world. They kept themselves free of urges and desires of the astral body that were directed only towards the world of the senses, and thus they became increasingly free of the astral body's errors. The conditions this brought about in them led them to perceive only with the part of the life body that was separate from the physical body. Under these conditions, the physical body's perceptive capacity was wiped out, so to speak, and the physical body itself seemed dead.

Through their life bodies, these human beings then united completely with the domain of the Spirits of Form, who showed them how they were being led and guided by the exalted being who had assumed leadership during the separation of sun and earth and who was later to make human beings receptive to understanding Christ. These individuals were initiates. However, because human individualities had entered the domain of the luciferic beings, as a rule even these initiates could not be directly touched by the great Sun Spirit, who could only be shown to them by the moon spirits as if in a reflection. They saw only the Sun Being's reflected glory.

These individuals became leaders of the other human beings and were able to communicate to them the Mysteries they had beheld. They attracted disciples whom they taught how to attain the state leading to initiation. Their knowledge, previously revealed through Christ, could be acquired only by people who were 'sun humanity' in the sense indicated above. They nurtured their mysterious knowledge and the practices that led to it in a special place which we can call the Christ Oracle or Sun Oracle — 'Oracle,' that is, in the sense of a place where the intentions of spiritual beings are perceived. What is said here about Christ will be misunderstood unless we consider the fact that supersensory knowledge necessarily sees the appearance of Christ on earth as an event that was foretold by those who were already aware of the meaning of the earth's evolution prior to this event. It would be a mistake to assume that these initiates had a relationship to Christ that would be possible only later, after his actual appearance on earth. However, they were able to grasp in a prophetic way and make comprehensible to their disciples that anyone touched by the power of the Sun Being sees Christ approaching the earth.

Other oracles were called into being by Saturn, Mars and Jupiter humans. The vision of the initiates of each group was directed upwards only as far as the being who could be discerned as the corresponding higher I in the life bodies of the members of their group. This is how the wisdom of Saturn, Jupiter and Mars acquired followers.

In addition to these methods of initiation, there were also methods for those who had absorbed too much of the luciferic principle, which prevented as large a part of their life body from separating from the physical body as was the case in sun humanity. In these people, the astral body retained more of the life body in the physical body, and they were incapable of being brought to a prophetic revelation of Christ by means of the conditions we have described. Because of the luciferic principle's greater influence on their astral bodies, they had to undergo more difficult preparations before being able, in a less body-free state than the others, to behold the other higher beings, though not Christ. Among the beings they were able to see, however, were certain ones who, although they had left the earth when the sun separated from it, were not yet at a level that would have permitted them to participate in the sun's evolution for any length of time. After the sun's separation from the earth, these beings pulled Venus out of the sun in order to make it their dwelling place. The being who became their leader also became the higher ego of the group of initiates and their followers described above. Something similar happened with the leading spirit of Mercury with regard to humans of a different type. This is how the Venus and Mercury Oracles came about.

Human beings of the particular type who had absorbed the most luciferic influence were able to reach up only as far as the leader of the beings who had been the first to be expelled from the sun's evolution. This being did not occupy a particular planet in cosmic space, but lived in the surroundings of the earth itself, having reunited with it after returning from the sun. This being manifested as the higher ego of human beings who can be called followers of the Vulcan Oracle. Their vision was directed more towards earthly phenomena than was the case with the other initiates, and they laid the first foundations for what later became the arts and sciences among human beings. In contrast, the Mercury initiates laid the basis for knowledge of more supersensory things, and the Venus initiates did this to an even greater extent. The fact that the Vulcan, Mercury and Venus initiates received their knowledge more in the form of their own thoughts and ideas distinguished them from the Saturn, Jupiter and Mars initiates, who received their Mysteries more as a revelation from above and in a more finished state. The Christ initiates occupied the middle ground, receiving the ability to clothe their Mysteries in human concepts along with their direct revelations. The Saturn, Jupiter and Mars initiates had to express themselves in symbols to a greater extent, while the Christ, Venus, Mercury and Vulcan initiates were more able to communicate through concepts.

What reached Atlantean humanity in this way happened indirectly, by way of the initiates. However, the rest of humankind also received special faculties as a result of the luciferic principle, because the exalted cosmic beings transformed certain faculties, that might otherwise have led to ruin, into a blessing. One such faculty was speech. Human beings received it as a result of the densification into physical, material nature and the separation of part of the life body from the physical body.

During the time following the moon's separation, human beings at first felt united with their physical ancestors through the 'group ego'. But this common consciousness connecting descendants and ancestors was gradually lost over the course of the generations. Later descendants had an inner memory that no longer reached back to their earlier ancestors, but only to not very distant ones. People's memories of one or the other ancestor appeared only during contact with the spiritual world in their sleeplike states. They were then likely to feel at one with their ancestors. They believed these ancestors had reappeared in themselves. This was an erroneous idea of reincarnation that emerged primarily in the last part of the Atlantean age. The truth about reincarnation could only be experienced in the schools of the initiates. Only the initiates, who saw human souls in the body-free state passing from one incarnation to another, were able to communicate the truth about this to their disciples.

At the point in the distant past that we are talking about here, the human physical figure was still very different from how it is now. To a great extent, it was still the expression of soul characteristics. Human beings still consisted of matter that was softer and more delicate than what they acquired later. What is solid today was then still soft, supple and malleable. Human beings with more pronounced soul and spiritual elements were delicate, mobile, and expressive in their bodily structure, while those who were spiritually less developed had body forms that were coarse, immobile and less malleable. Advancement on a soul level contracted the limbs and kept a person's stature small, while delayed soul development and entanglement in sensuality expressed itself in gigantic size. During their growth period, people's bodies took shape according to what was forming in their souls in a way that seems incredible or even fantastic to our modern way of looking at things. Moral depravity in a person's passions, drives, and instincts resulted in a gigantic increase in material substance.

Our present human physical form came about through contracting, densifying and solidifying the Atlantean one. Prior to the Atlantean age, human beings were faithful copies of their soul character, but the causes that led to the post-Atlantean human form, which is solid and relatively independent of any soul qualities, were inherent in the processes of Atlantean evolution. (The animal kingdom on earth became dense in its forms much earlier than human beings.) Under no circumstances can the laws currently governing the way that forms take shape in the kingdoms of nature be extended to the distant past.

Towards the middle of the Atlantean age, a great disaster was gradually building up within humankind. The secrets of the initiates should have been carefully protected from individuals who had not prepared their astral bodies to receive this knowledge by cleansing them of error. When such people did acquire an insight into this hidden knowledge, into the laws through which higher beings guided the forces of nature, they used these laws for purposes that served their aberrant needs and obsessions. The danger became even greater when these people entered the domain of the lower spiritual beings who could not participate in the earth's normal evolution and worked against it. These beings were constantly influencing human beings by promoting interests that actually worked contrary to human benefit.

At that time, human beings still had the ability to use the natural growth and reproductive forces of animals and humans for their own purposes. Not only ordinary people but also some initiates succumbed to the temptations provided by the lower spiritual beings and used these supersensory forces in the service of aims that ran counter to humanity's evolution. To carry this out, they chose associates who were not initiates and who used the mysteries of nature's supersensory workings exclusively for baser purposes. The consequence was great corruption among humankind. The evil spread further and further, and since the forces of growth and reproduction when uprooted and applied out of context have a mysterious connection to certain forces at work in air and water, these human actions released powerfully destructive natural forces. This led to the gradual destruction of the Atlantean region through catastrophes involving the earth's air and water.

The Atlanteans—at least those who did not perish in the storms—were forced to emigrate. The storms were changing the entire face of the earth. Europe, Asia and Africa on one side and America on the other were gradually acquiring the shapes they have today. Vast numbers of emigrants headed for these lands. As far as our present situation is concerned, the most important migrations were the ones that moved eastward from Atlantis. Europe, Asia and Africa were gradually settled by descendants of the Atlanteans. Various peoples differing in their degrees of both development and corruption took up residence there. In their midst marched the initiates, who guarded the Mysteries of the oracles and established centres in various regions where the services of Jupiter, Venus, and so on, were cultivated in both the good sense and the bad.

The betrayal of the Vulcan Mysteries had an especially

negative effect,[17] because their followers' view was the most focused on earthly circumstances. This betrayal forced human beings to become dependent on spiritual beings whose prior development made them reject everything coming from the spiritual world that had evolved as a result of the earth's separation from the sun. As a result of this, these beings worked specifically in the human element that resulted from having sensory perceptions that drew a veil over the spiritual element. From this point onward, these beings acquired a great deal of influence over many of the earth's human inhabitants. This influence first made itself felt in the fact that human beings were increasingly deprived of the feeling for the spiritual.

Since the size, form and flexibility of the human physical body were still to a very great extent determined by soul qualities during this period, the betrayal of the Mysteries also came to light in corresponding changes in the human race. Amorphous human figures, grotesque in both size and shape, were created wherever human corruption was especially evident, wherever supersensory forces were placed in the service of baser drives, desires and passions.[18] Such figures, however, could not persist beyond the actual Atlantean period. They died out. Physically, post-Atlantean humankind developed from Atlantean ancestors whose bodily forms had already solidified in a way that did not allow them to succumb to soul forces that were contrary to nature.

There was a certain period in Atlantean evolution when the laws prevailing in and around the earth resulted in conditions that forced human forms to solidify. Although the races of humanity that had already solidified before this period were able to continue reproducing for a long time, their bodies gradually grew so restricting for the souls incarnating into them that these races were forced to die out. In actual fact, some of these racial forms persisted into post-Atlantean times, and modified forms of the ones that remained sufficiently flexible continued to exist for a very long time. However, the ones among them that did remain flexible beyond this time tended to embody souls that had experienced the damaging influence of the betrayal of the Mysteries to a very great extent. These forms were destined to die out quickly.

Thus, ever since the middle of the Atlantean age, beings had been present who exerted their influence in human evolution by making human beings live their way into the physical world of the senses in an unspiritual way. This went so far that people saw phantasmagoric delusions and illusions of all sorts instead of the true form of this world. However, human beings were exposed not only to the luciferic influence, but also to the influence of those other beings we have spoken about, whose leader can be called Ahriman. (This is the name that was given to this being later on during the ancient Iranian civilization. Mephistopheles is the same being.) Through this influence, human beings who had died fell into the hands of powers that made them appear like beings exclusively inclined towards earthly, sensory circumstances. They were increasingly deprived of their free view into the processes of the spiritual world. They were made to feel that they were in Ahriman's power and were excluded from the fellowship of the spiritual world to a certain extent.

One especially significant Oracle preserved the ancient service in the purest form amid the general decline. It was one of the Christ Oracles, and for that reason was able to preserve not only the Mystery of Christ but also the Mysteries of the other oracles, since revelation of the most exalted Sun Spirit also disclosed the leading spirits of Saturn, Jupiter, and so on. The initiates of this Sun Oracle knew the secret of how to generate in certain human beings the types of life body that had been possessed by the best initiates of Jupiter, Mercury, and so on. With the means at their disposal, which cannot be discussed further here, they effectively perpetuated reproductions of the best life bodies of ancient initiates and implanted them later in suitable individuals. The Venus, Mercury and Vulcan initiates made it possible for similar processes to take place with regard to astral bodies.

In a certain period, the leading Christ initiate found himself isolated with a few associates who were only capable of receiving the secrets of the cosmos to a very limited extent, because they were naturally predisposed to having physical and life bodies with the least degree of separation between them. At that time, such individuals were the best ones to assure the further progress of humankind. Because they experienced less and less during the sleeping state, the spiritual world was increasingly closed to them and they lacked all understanding of what had been revealed in ancient times when human beings occupied only life bodies rather than physical bodies. The individuals in the immediate environment of this leader of the Christ Oracle were the most advanced with regard to the reunification of the physical body with that portion of the life body that was formerly separate from it. This reunification was gradually being accomplished among human beings as a consequence of changes that had taken place in their Atlantean home and on earth in general. Human physical and life bodies were coinciding to an ever greater extent.

As a result of this, human beings lost their previously boundless faculty of memory, and human thought life began. The part of the life body that was united with the physical body transformed the physical brain into the actual instrument of thinking. Only after this did human beings actually experience the ego within the physical body. Self-awareness awakened for the first time. To begin with, this was actually true of only a small percentage of human beings, primarily associates of the leader of the Christ Oracle. The mass of human beings scattered across Europe, Asia and Africa preserved the remnants of older states of consciousness to varying degrees and therefore experienced the supersensory world directly.

The Christ initiate's associates were people of highly developed intellect, but of all the people living at that time, they had the least experience in the supersensory domain. This initiate moved with them from the west to the east, to an area in Central Asia, wanting to protect them as much as possible from contact with human beings of less advanced consciousness. He educated these associates of his, and more especially their descendants, in accordance with the Mysteries that were revealed to him. Thus, he trained a whole host of human beings who took to heart impulses that were in harmony with the Mysteries of the Christ initiation. From among them, he selected the seven best to receive life bodies and astral bodies that were reproductions of those of the seven greatest Atlantean initiates. In this way he educated one successor for each of the initiates of Christ, Saturn, Jupiter, and so on. These seven new initiates became the teachers and leaders of the human beings who had settled in the southern part of Asia, specifically in ancient India. Since these great teachers were actually endowed with reproductions of the life bodies of their spiritual ancestors, what was present in their astral bodies, namely, the knowledge and understanding they had assimilated themselves, did not extend to what was revealed to them through their life bodies. If this revelation was to speak in them, they had to silence their own knowledge and understanding. When they did so, the exalted beings who had spoken to their spiritual ancestors also spoke through them and out of them. Other than at the times when such beings were speaking through them, these were simple people gifted with whatever degree of intellectual and emotional education they had acquired on their own.

The origin of the Mysteries

At that time, India was occupied by human beings who had markedly preserved a living memory of the ancient Atlan-

tean state of soul that had permitted experience in the
spiritual world. A large number of these people also possessed a very strong tendency of heart and mind to want to
experience this supersensory world. Due to the wise guidance of destiny, the majority of people of this type, who
came from the best portions of the Atlantean population, had
migrated to southern Asia. In addition to this majority,
others had immigrated at different times. The Christ initiate
mentioned above appointed his seven greatest disciples to be
the teachers of this association of human beings, to give their
wisdom and their commandments to this group of people.

For many of these ancient Indians, very little preparation
was required to bring to life in them the barely extinguished
faculties that led to observation of the supersensory world,
because a longing for this world was actually a fundamental
mood of Indian souls. They felt that the original home of
human beings was in this supersensory world, that they had
been transplanted from this world to the world that can be
provided by outer sensory perception and the sense-bound
intellect. They felt that the supersensory world was the true
one and that the sensory world was *maya,* an illusion of
human perception. They strove by all possible means to open
a view into the spiritual world. They were unable to develop
any interest in the illusory world of the senses, or only to the
extent that it proved to be a veil over the supersensory world.
The power that the seven great teachers (rishis) could exert
on people like this was tremendous, and what they revealed
made its way deep into Indian souls. And because the life
bodies and astral bodies that had been passed down to them

bestowed sublime powers on these teachers, they were able to have magical effects on their disciples. They did not actually teach, but their personalities acted upon those of others as if through magical powers. The civilization that came about in this way was completely imbued with supersensory wisdom.

What is contained in the *Vedas*, the books of Indian wisdom, is not the original form of the exalted wisdom fostered by these great teachers in ancient times, but only a feeble echo of it. Only supersensory sight can look back to the original unrecorded wisdom behind what was written. An especially prominent characteristic of this original wisdom is the harmony and accord that existed among the various Oracles of Atlantean times. Each of the great teachers could divulge the wisdom of one of the Oracles, and these various aspects of wisdom were in complete harmony, because the fundamental wisdom of the initiation that prophesied the coming of Christ stood behind all of them. However, the teacher who was the spiritual successor of the Christ initiate did not present what this initiate himself, who had remained in the background of evolution, was capable of revealing. Initially, it was not possible for the Atlantean Christ initiate to pass on his high office to any post-Atlantean individual. In contrast to the Atlantean Christ initiate, who was able completely to transmute his perception of the Christ mystery into human concepts, the Indian Christ initiate was only capable of presenting a reflection of this mystery in signs and symbols, because his humanly acquired conceptual abilities could not encompass this mystery.

Nonetheless, the result of the union of the seven teachers was a panorama of wisdom expressing their knowledge of the supersensory world, only parts of which could have been promulgated in the old Atlantean Oracle. This panorama revealed the exalted leadership of the cosmic world and quietly alluded to a great Sun Spirit, the concealed being who was enthroned above the beings revealed by the seven teachers.

What the term 'ancient Indians' means here is not what is usually understood by it. No outer documents have come down to us from the time we are speaking of here. The nation of people now known as Indians belongs to a historical stage of evolution that came about only much later than this. We must recognize the 'Indian' culture described here as the prevailing culture of the first post-Atlantean epoch in the earth's history.[19] After that came a second post-Atlantean epoch, when the 'ancient Iranian' civilization described later on in this book was the dominant culture. Still later, the Egypto-Mesopotamian civilization developed. It too will be described later. While the second and third post-Atlantean cultural epochs were taking shape, the 'ancient' Indian culture also underwent its own second and third periods. The third period is what is commonly described as 'ancient India'. We must not confuse what is described here with the historical ancient India spoken of elsewhere.

What later led to separating people into castes was another characteristic of the culture of ancient India. The inhabitants of India were descendants of Atlanteans who had belonged to different human types: the Saturn humans, Jupiter humans, and so on. Through supersensory teaching, they understood that a soul's position in a certain caste was not a matter of coincidence but a matter of self-determination. The fact that many people were able to stir up inner memories of their ancestors, as described earlier, made it easier for them to understand supersensory teachings in this way, but it also easily led to erroneous ideas about reincarnation. During the Atlantean age, the truth about reincarnation could only be acquired through the initiates. Similarly, during the earliest Indian times this truth could only be acquired through direct contact with the great teachers. In fact, the mistaken concept of reincarnation that was described earlier was extremely prevalent among the people who had spread out over Europe, Asia and Africa after the sinking of Atlantis. And because initiates who had gone astray during the Atlantean evolutionary period had also shared this mystery with people who were not ready to receive it, people increasingly confused the correct idea with the false one. Many of these people still possessed a dim kind of clairvoyance as a legacy of the Atlantean age. While the Atlanteans entered the domain of the spiritual world during sleep, their descendants experienced this spiritual world in abnormal intermediate states between waking and sleeping. In these states, images of an older time to which their ancestors had belonged appeared in them, so they considered themselves reincarnations of people who had lived in those times. Teachings about reincarnation that contradicted the initiates' genuine ideas on the subject spread over the entire earth.

Ongoing migrations from west to east since the beginning

of the destruction of Atlantis led to the settlement of the Middle East by a group of people whose descendants went down in history as the Iranians and their affiliated tribes. Supersensory cognition, however, must look much further back in time than the recorded history of these ethnic groups. We must first speak about the later Iranians' very distant ancestors, who issued in the second great epoch of civilization in post-Atlantean evolution. It came about after the Indian civilization. The people of this second epoch had a different task from the Indians. Their inclinations and longings were not directed only at the supersensory world but were also adapted to the physical world of the senses. They began to love the earth. They valued what human beings could conquer for themselves on earth and what they could gain through earthly forces. Their accomplishments as a warrior nation and the methods they invented for extracting the earth's treasures are related to this characteristic of their nature. There was no danger that their longing for the supersensory would turn them completely away from the 'illusion' of the physical, sense-perceptible world. On the contrary, they were more in danger of completely losing their souls' connection to the supersensory world because of their appreciation for the physical world.

The character of the Oracles that had been transplanted from Atlantis also reflected the general character of the people. Formerly, human beings had been able to acquire certain powers by experiencing the supersensory world. In that time, it was still possible to control some lower forms of these powers. Of these powers, there were those cultivated in the oracles that guided natural phenomena in ways that served personal human interests. These ancient people still had great ability to control forces in nature that later retreated beyond the reach of human will. The guardians of the Oracles, who had inner forces at their command that were related to fire and other elements, can be called 'Magi' or magicians. The legacy of supersensory knowledge and supersensory forces that they had preserved for themselves, although insignificant in comparison to what human beings had been capable of in the still more distant past, appeared in many different forms, ranging from the noblest arts whose only purpose was the welfare of human beings to the most reprehensible practices. The luciferic principle prevailed in these people in a very particular way, connecting them with everything that could distract human beings from the intentions of those higher beings who would have been the sole guides of human progress if the luciferic intervention had not happened. Even the members of this people who were still gifted with remnants of the ancient clairvoyant state, the intermediary state between waking and sleeping that was described earlier, felt very drawn to the lower beings of the spiritual world. Because these people needed a spiritual impetus that would counteract this character trait in them, they were supplied with leadership by what had also been the source of ancient Indian spiritual life, namely, the guardian of the mysteries of the Sun Oracle.

For these people, the guardian of the Sun Oracle provided a leader who can be referred to by the name that has come down to us in history as Zarathustra or Zoroaster, but it must be emphasized that the person we are speaking about here belonged to a much earlier age than the historical bearer of that name. However, we are dealing here with a question of spiritual science rather than one of outer historical research. Anyone who cannot help but think of a later age in connection with the bearer of the name Zarathustra can reconcile this with spiritual science by thinking of the historical Zarathustra as a successor to the first great Zarathustra, as someone who assumed his name and worked in the spirit of his teaching.[20]

The impulse Zarathustra needed to provide for his people consisted in pointing out that the physical world of the senses is more than just the spiritless thing people encounter when they fall exclusively under the influence of the being of Lucifer. Human beings owe their personal independence and their sense of freedom to this being. However, Lucifer is supposed to work in them in harmony with the opposite spiritual principle. It was important for the ancient Iranian people to remain alert to the presence of this other spiritual being. Their inclination towards the physical world of the senses threatened to make them merge completely with the luciferic beings.

Now, the initiation Zarathustra had received through the guardian of the Sun Oracle allowed him to receive the revelations of the exalted sun beings. His training had led him to special states of consciousness in which he was able to behold the sun beings' leader, who had taken the human ether body under his protection as previously described. Zarathustra knew that this being was guiding the evolution of humanity but would only be able to descend to earth from cosmic space at a certain point in the future. For this to happen, this being would have to be able to live in the astral body of a human being in the same way that he had been able to work in the human life body ever since the luciferic intervention took place. For this to happen, a human being would have to appear who had transformed the astral body back to the stage it would have attained without Lucifer at a certain other point in time (in the middle of the Atlantean period of evolution). Without Lucifer, human beings would have reached this stage earlier, but without personal independence and without the possibility of freedom. From this point onwards, however, human beings were to regain this high level in spite of these traits of their character. In his clairvoyant states, Zarathustra saw that in humankind's future evolution it would be possible for a specific person to have an astral body of this sort. He also knew that until this time arrived, it was impossible to find the spiritual forces of the sun on earth; they could be perceived, however, by means of supersensory sight in the domain of the spiritual portion of the sun. He was able to see these forces when he turned his clairvoyant gaze towards the sun, and he brought his people tidings of the nature of these forces, which at that time could be found only in the spiritual world but would later descend to earth. In this way he proclaimed the great Spirit of the Sun, the Spirit of Light (the sun aura, Ahura-Mazda or Ohrmazd). For Zarathustra and his followers, this Spirit of Light became manifest as the spirit who turns his countenance towards human beings from the spiritual world and prepares the future within humankind. This spirit, who points to the Christ before his appearance on earth, was the spirit Zarathustra proclaimed as the Spirit of Light.

In contrast, Zarathustra depicted Ahriman (Angra Mainyu) as a power whose influence causes the human soul life to deteriorate when it surrenders to this influence in a one-sided way. This power is none other than the one described earlier as having achieved a particular dominion over the earth ever since the betrayal of the Vulcan Mysteries. Alongside his tidings of the Light God, Zarathustra also proclaimed the doctrine concerning spiritual beings that reveal themselves to the purified consciousness of the seer as the companions of the Spirit of Light. In stark contrast to these beings were the tempters who were appearing to the unpurified remnants of clairvoyance that had been retained from Atlantean times. It had to be made clear to the ancient Iranians that the human soul, to the extent that it was inclined towards working and striving in the physical world of the senses, was the battleground in a conflict between the power of the Light God and that of his adversary. Zarathustra showed how human beings had to act so as not to be led into the abyss by this adversary, whose influence might be turned to good through the power of the Spirit of Light.

A third post-Atlantean cultural epoch first developed among the peoples who eventually migrated into the Middle East and North Africa—the Babylonians and Assyrians of Mesopotamia on the one hand and the Egyptians on the other. They developed a still different understanding of the physical, sense-perceptible world from the ancient Iranians. In comparison to other ethnic groups, they had acquired much more of a spiritual predisposition for intellectual endowment, for the ability to think that had been developing since the later part of the Atlantean age. As we know, it was the task of post-Atlantean humanity to develop soul faculties that could be acquired through awakened powers of thought and feeling that are not directly stimulated by the spiritual world but come about when human beings observe the world of the senses, find their way into it, and adapt it. Conquering the physical world with these human faculties must be seen as the mission of post-Atlantean humanity.

This conquest proceeded step by step. In ancient India, people still saw the physical world as an illusion although their soul make-up already directed them towards it, and their spirits turned towards the supersensory world. In contrast, the ancient Iranian people began an attempt to conquer the physical world of the senses, but to a large extent they still did so with soul forces that were the legacy of a time when human beings could reach directly into the super-sensory world. Among the peoples of the third cultural epoch, souls had lost much of their supersensory faculties. They had to investigate the spirit's manifestations in their sense-perceptible environment; their progress came from discovering and inventing the cultural means of advance-ment that this environment yielded. Humankind's sciences came about through deriving the laws of the spiritual world from the physical sense-world that concealed it; technology and the arts and their tools and methods came about through recognizing and applying the forces of this sensory world. The Mesopotamians and Babylonians no longer saw the world of the senses as an illusion. They saw its natural kingdoms, its mountains and seas, its air and water, as manifestations of the spiritual deeds of powers standing behind this world, and they attempted to discover the laws governing these powers. To the Egyptians, the earth was the setting for their work. In the state in which it was given to them, it was in need of being transformed through their own intellectual forces so that it would reflect the impact of human power.

The Oracles that had been transplanted from Atlantis to Egypt originated primarily in the Atlantean Mercury Oracle, but there were also others—the Venus Oracles, for example. What these Oracles cultivated in the Egyptian people became the seed of a new civilization. This seed originated with a great leader who had been trained in the Iranian mysteries of Zarathustra and was a reincarnation of one of the disciples of the great Zarathustra himself. If we want to cite a historical name, we can call him Hermes.[21] Through absorbing the Zarathustrian Mysteries, he was able to find the right way to guide the Egyptian people. In earthly life between birth and death, the Egyptians approached the physical world of the senses with their understanding in a way that allowed them to perceive the spiritual world behind the world of the senses only to a very limited extent; however, they were able to recognize spiritual laws in the sense-perceptible world. Therefore, they could not be taught about this spiritual world as one they would be able to enter during life on earth, but it was possible to show them how human beings in the body-free state after death would commune with the world of spirits that left impressions in the sense-perceptible, physical domain during an earthly human lifetime. Hermes taught that to the extent that human beings on earth applied their forces to working in accordance with the intentions of spiritual powers, they make it possible for them to unite with these powers after death. In particular, those who had worked most diligently in this direction between birth and death would be united with Osiris, the exalted Sun being.

The Mesopotamian-Babylonian aspect of this cultural stream was more emphatic than the Egyptian in directing the human mind towards the physical world of the senses. The laws of this world were investigated and spiritual archetypes were perceived in their sense-perceptible images. However, in many respects this people remained caught in the sense-perceptible element. Instead of a star spirit, the star was pushed into the foreground, and the same was true of other spiritual beings and their earthly manifestations. Only their leaders acquired really deep knowledge of the laws of the supersensory world and of how these laws worked together with the sense world. The contrast between the knowledge of the initiates and the mistaken beliefs of the people was stronger here than anywhere else.

Conditions were quite different in the areas of southern Europe and the Middle East where the fourth post-Atlantean cultural epoch blossomed. We can call this the Graeco-Latin epoch. The migrants to these countries were the descendants of people from many different parts of the ancient world, and their Oracles followed the traditions of many different Atlantean Oracles. Some individuals possessed the legacy of ancient clairvoyance as a natural faculty; for others, it was relatively easy to acquire it through training. Particular centres not only preserved what had come down from the ancient initiates but also developed worthy successors, who in turn trained disciples who were capable of rising to high levels of spiritual perception. This meant that these ethnic groups possessed an inner urge to create a place in the sense-perceptible world that would express the spiritual element in its perfect form within the physical element.

This urge resulted in Greek art, among many other things. If we can grasp a Greek temple through spiritual sight, we will recognize that in this marvellous work of art human beings have transformed the sense-perceptible, material element in such a way that every part of it has become an expression of the spiritual. A Greek temple is the 'house of the spirit'. In beholding its forms, we perceive what is otherwise seen only by seers. A temple of Zeus (or Jupiter) is fashioned in a way that presents our physical sense of sight with a worthy vessel for what the guardian of the Zeus or Jupiter initiation beheld with spiritual sight. This is true of all Greek art.

In mysterious ways, the wisdom of the initiates flowed into poets, artists and thinkers. In the constructs of ancient Greek philosophy, the Mystery wisdom of the initiates is found again in the form of concepts and ideas. The influence of the spiritual life, the Mysteries of the Asian and African initiation centres, flowed into these people and their leaders.

The great Indian teachers, the associates of Zarathustra, and the followers of Hermes had all trained disciples, and either these disciples or their successors then founded initiation centres in which the ancient wisdom came to life in a new form. These were the Mysteries of antiquity, where disciples were prepared to reach states of consciousness that would allow them to attain perception of the spiritual world. (Further details concerning these Mysteries are available in my book *Christianity as Mystical Fact*.[22]) Wisdom flowed out of these initiation centres to those who cultivated the Mysteries of the spirit in Ionia, mainland Greece, and Italy. In the Greek-speaking world, the Orphic and Eleusinian Mysteries developed into important initiation centres. The great teachings and methods of wisdom from earlier times worked on in the Pythagorean school of wisdom because Pythagoras had been initiated into the secrets of a variety of Mysteries during his extensive travels.

6. Concluding Survey: Atlantis and Spiritual Evolution

Widening the perspective still further, Rudolf Steiner surveys in an extraordinarily far-seeing manner the whole sweep of humanity's evolution. Almost apocalyptic in scope, his vision nevertheless remains true to the principle from which he started out, being grounded in the inner connections between human consciousness and the greater world, the macrocosm, in which it evolved. Far from being exhausted, the potentialities of human consciousness still point to even more significant transformations of our world in the future.

The first human beings appeared comparatively late in the earth's evolution and at that time they had a very different constitution from the present. I cannot describe to you the forms of those human beings which first crystallized, so to speak, out of the spirit. Although you have already heard much that is difficult to believe, you would be too greatly shocked if I were to describe to you the grotesque forms of the bodies in which your souls were then incarnated. You would not be able to bear such a description. However, at a later date, when these things which are only now beginning to come to the consciousness of people through anthroposophy, when they increasingly penetrate people's consciousness, this will have to be made known, and it will have a tremendous result, it will be extremely important to the whole life of human beings. For only when human beings learn how their bodies have developed, how the organs they now possess have gradually developed out of entirely different forms, will they feel that remarkable relationship which exists between organs in the human body which today are apparently far apart.

They will then see the correspondence between certain organs, for example between the appendix and the windpipe, which in their earlier form grew together in those remarkably formed beings. All that is human being today is the previous form unrolled, as it were, the previous form unfolded in the most varied ways. Organs which today are separated formerly grew together. They have, however, kept their relationship, and very frequently this relationship is manifested in illnesses. It is seen that when a certain organ is diseased another one becomes diseased in consequence. Hence those who really study medicine will have to make many discoveries of which present-day medicine, which is only a collection of notes, has no inkling; only then will physicians really learn something about the true nature of man. All this is merely to point out how entirely different people's earlier form was.

The solid parts were only built into this human form gradually. There were originally no bones in the human body, even when it had already descended. The bones developed out of soft cartilaginous structures which traversed the human body like cords. These in turn originated

from quite soft substances, and these soft substances from
fluid ones, the fluid from airy ones, the airy from etheric ones
and the etheric from astral ones which had densified from
spiritual substantiality. If you trace it back, you will find that
everything material has originated from the spirit. Everything already exists in the spiritual world. It was only in the
Atlantean epoch that the bones, which previously existed
only in predisposed form, actually developed in human
beings. We must now examine Lemurian mankind more
closely. We will then understand the writer of the Apocalypse better.[23] I need only indicate that following the first
period when the moon had separated from the earth and
human beings descended, their will was very different in
nature from what it became later. At that time the will of
human beings worked magically — it could affect the growth
of flowers. When they exerted their will, they could make a
flower shoot up quickly, a capacity which can only be
acquired today by an abnormal process of development.
Hence at that time the natural surroundings depended upon
how the human will was constituted. If it was good it
worked soothingly upon the billowing waters, upon the
storm and upon the fiery structures that were then all
around, for the earth was to a great extent of a volcanic
nature. Human beings worked soothingly upon all this by
means of good will and destructively by means of evil will.
Thus the human will was in complete correspondence with
its environment. The land masses upon which human beings
then lived were destroyed essentially by the evil will of
human beings, and only a small part of humankind saved

itself (we have again here to distinguish between race development and soul development) into our epoch, an epoch which we can describe in proper words because we can now find terms in our language that are adequate for the depiction of what clairvoyant consciousness perceives.

After this catastrophe we come to the ancient Atlantean epoch when the human race developed on a continent which now forms the bed of the Atlantic Ocean, between the present Europe and America. At that time human beings lived under very different physical conditions. At the beginning of the Atlantean epoch they were a structure which perceived in quite a different way from present human beings.

They still had a kind of spiritual vision, because the construction of their bodies was different from what it is now. The etheric body was not yet so firmly bound up with the physical body. The etheric body of the head extended far beyond the physical body. Only towards the last third of the Atlantean epoch did the projecting etheric body draw in and take the form of the present physical human head. Since the form of the ancient Atlanteans was so very different from that of present human beings and the parts of their being were so differently joined together, their whole consciousness, their whole soul life was also different. And here — if we wish to understand the writer of the Apocalypse — we must touch upon a very important, but a very mysterious, chapter. If you were to enter this ancient Atlantis, you would find that it was surrounded not by such pure air as the present earth but by air saturated with volumes of mist, with water. This air became clearer and more transparent the further Atlantis

developed, but the mists were densest where the more
advanced Atlantean civilization developed. That is where
the thickest mists were, and from these the foundations of
the later cultures developed. Atlantis was covered far and
wide by these mists. A division of rain and sunshine such as
we have today did not then exist. Hence in ancient Atlantis
what you know as the rainbow could not appear. You might
search the whole of Atlantis and you would hardly find it.
Only when the condensation of the water led to flooding,
when the great Flood spread itself over the earth, could the
rainbow come into being physically. And this is a point
where on the basis of spiritual science you will gain the
greatest respect for the religious records. For when you are
told that after the Flood, Noah, the representative of those
who saved mankind, sees the rainbow first appear, this is
really an historical event. After the Flood, mankind saw the
first rainbow; previously it was an impossibility — simply
from the point of view of physics.

Here you can see how profound, how literally true the
religious records are today.[24] Many people are distressed
when one says that the religious records are literally true.
Many quote a saying which is true; it is quoted, however, by
lazy people, not as a true statement but because they are lazy.
It is the saying: 'The letter killeth but the spirit giveth life'.
From this they deduce the right to take no notice at all of
what is written in the records, no longer to need to recognize
what the records actually say, for they are the 'dead letter',
they claim. And so they like to let their intellect shine and
concoct all sorts of fantasies. These persons may indeed be

very clever in their explanations, but that is not the point; the point is that we ought really to see in the records what they contain. 'The letter killeth but the spirit giveth life' has the same significance in mystical language as Goethe's saying

If you have not this in you:
'Die and then become again!'
You are but a sombre guest
On earth's dark and gloomy plane.

This saying does not mean: if you wish to lead someone to a higher knowledge you must slay him. It means that it is precisely through the culture of the physical world that human beings must uplift themselves to spirituality. In the same way the letter is the body of the spirit, and we must first possess and understand the letter, then we may say that we can find the spirit in it. The letter, the understood letter, must then die so that the spirit may be resurrected from it. This saying is not an injunction to fancy anything you please about what is contained in the religious records. When we recognize the true significance of the rainbow as we have represented it, something like deep respect for the religious records penetrates our soul, and we gain an idea of how, through a deeper knowledge based on anthroposophy, human beings attain a true and genuine feeling for religious documents and a truly purposeful understanding of them.

Let us now look back to ancient Atlantis. We have already said that man then lived in a different state of consciousness and that his memory was different from what it is now; but the difference is much greater. If we go far back not merely into the later period of Atlantis but to the beginning, we find a human consciousness very different from what we possess today.

Let us once more consider our present consciousness. During the day a person uses his senses. At night he goes to sleep. In his bed lie the physical body and the etheric body; the astral body and the ego withdraw. The sphere of consciousness darkens. Human beings today see nothing and hear nothing. Then, in the morning, when the astral body and the ego re-enter the physical body and etheric body, physical objects once more confront them. How was it in the early Atlantean age? Let us take the moment when in the morning human beings plunged into their physical and etheric bodies; at that time they did not find a physical world around them such as we have today. All the present objects which are now seen with clear outlines were then seen as if surrounded with an aura, with coloured edges, quite indistinctly. In ancient Atlantis the appearance was somewhat similar to what is now seen when in the evening there is a dense fog and you see the street lamps not clearly, but surrounded by coloured edges. Thus it was in early Atlantis. All objects were seen indistinctly, not with clear outlines and surfaces as today; everything was as if enveloped in coloured mist. Only gradually have clear outlines developed. Had we looked at a rose in the first part of Atlantis, it would have been as if a cloudy structure arose with a red disc in the middle. Only gradually did the external colour appear to be laid on the surface; only later did objects obtain sharp outlines.

Hence you see that the physical world surrounding human beings was quite different in ancient Atlantis. It was also different when at night they rose out of their physical body when—shall we say—they went to sleep. Really it was not sleep in the present sense. The entire world of the misty physical formations remained below, and a spiritual world arose. Possessing no sharp outlines, human beings lived within a spiritual world. Spiritual beings were their companions. In the first part of the Atlantean age, day and night alternated in such a way that when human beings plunged into their physical bodies they had only hazy, indistinct pictures of the physical world; but when at night they left their physical bodies they were able to live spiritually, although somewhat indistinctly, among spirits; they moved among spirits. And above all, people's entire life of feeling was also different in the Atlantean epoch. At that time, when they went out of their physical and etheric bodies, they did not feel fatigue and the need for rest. Neither did they find rest. They had to enter into the spiritual world; that was then their sphere of activity. On the other hand, when the morning came, they felt the need for rest and sought out their resting place, which was their own body. There they lay peacefully. They crept into their own body and rested during the day.

Thus in the first period of Atlantis things were entirely different from now. During the Atlantean epoch, a process took place in which human beings gradually passed from one set of conditions into their opposite. This was caused by the etheric body increasingly being driven into the physical body and occurred during the last third of the Atlantean epoch. Before this event, human beings felt themselves as waking beings above in the spiritual world; but as such they did not say 'I' to themselves, they did not possess consciousness of self. When they withdrew from their physical and etheric bodies in order to go into the brilliance of the night, they felt themselves to be members of the spiritual world which was above; they felt themselves safely protected, one might say, in their group soul. It always became bright around them during the night; but they felt themselves to be dependent on that world. Just as our finger belongs to our ego, so human beings felt that they belonged to the group souls which are represented clairvoyantly as the four heads of the lion, eagle, bull and man described in the Apocalypse of St John. Human beings felt themselves transposed into one such group soul. And only when, snail-like, they were in their bodily shells did they feel that they possessed something of their own. For the reason that humans developed as independent beings was the result of their being able to envelop themselves in their bodies. They had, however, to pay for this confinement in their bodies with the gradual obscuration of the spiritual world until it had completely withdrawn. In its place the world which they saw below when they were in their physical bodies became brighter and clearer. In this way it gradually dawned upon them that they were egos, that they had consciousness of self within themselves. They learned to say 'I' to themselves.

If we wish to characterize what took place at that time, we must imagine human beings creeping out of their 'snail-shells' into the spiritual world. There they were among spiritual, divine beings. There they hear from outside themselves the name of what they are. One group heard the word which in the original language was the word for that group; another group heard a different word. Human beings could not name themselves from within; their name sounded into them from without. When they thus crept out of the 'snail-shell' of their body, they knew what they were because this knowledge was intoned into their souls. Then, when in their body they learned to perceive the physical environment, they learned to feel themselves as an I; they learned to feel within themselves the divine power which had previously sounded to them from outside. They learned to feel God within themselves. The god who was closest to them, who referred to their ego, they called Yahveh. This god was the guide of their ego, and human beings felt the power of this god arising within their ego.

External events were associated with this. When the ancient Atlanteans thus descended into their physical bodies and looked out into space, they did not see an actual rainbow; in the place where the sun later emerged, they saw something like a circle formed of colour. The sun did not yet penetrate with its power but made itself felt through the mist. Though hindered and held back by the fog, its forces influenced the earth. It appeared very gradually. Thus all that we have described as the awakening of external consciousness was connected with the emergence of the sun from the mist. What existed up above where the six other spirits, who together with Yahveh guided earth evolution, had their abode gradually emerged and shone down upon the earth in deeds.

What had taken place in human beings? When previously they rose out of their bodies, when it was 'night', their soul and spirit entered into the inner astral brilliance, which does not require the external sun. This brilliance surrounded them. It was the same light from mighty spiritual beings which later shone down physically from the sun. As they gradually enclosed themselves more and more in their physical consciousness, the door of inner vision was closed. Darkness surrounded them when at night they left their physical and etheric bodies and entered the spiritual world. The external light, representing the deeds of the spiritual beings of the sun, grew to the same extent to which human beings became confined; the light of the spiritual beings shone externally on the earth. Human beings prepared themselves to look upon the external light as something material. The light shone in his darkened inner being, but the light was not at that time comprehended by his darkness.

This is a cosmic process in world history. Human beings acquired consciousness of self through spiritual darkening. In this way human beings grew away from the brilliance of the group souls. But it was only the very first dawning of individuality. It was a long, long time before they really grew to possess it. The last period of the Atlantean age passed away and the Flood came. The post-Atlantean epoch began. Ancient Indian culture passed away. True consciousness of self had not yet developed. Then came the Iranian and Babylonian-Egyptian ages. Human beings gradually

*In this pastel sketch by Rudolf Steiner, the working of cosmic forces into the
still heavy and mist-laden atmosphere of Atlantis is shown as guided by
god-like angelic beings. Out of the downward streaming colours are born
the types of the lion, cow, and bird (left), while to the right a kind of cave
unfolds inner life and form. (Preliminary sketch for the large cupola of the
Goetheanum ceiling, Dornach, Switzerland).*

matured in order to develop an inner consciousness of self. At length, the fourth age arrived. At this stage something of tremendous importance took place, which had been prepared by all that had previously happened.

Imagine yourself now uplifted from the earth to a distant star and gifted with clairvoyant vision, looking down to the earth from that distant star. You would then see that this earth as a physical body is just that, and that an etheric body and an astral body belong to it, just as with human beings. The earth has all this too. You would see the earth surrounded by its aura and from that star you would be able to follow the development of the earth's aura over thousands of years. You would see the earth surrounded by all sorts of colours: in the centre the physical kernel and around it the aura floating in various forms and colours. This spiritual atmosphere of the earth would reveal many different structures. You would see these colours and forms change in various ways in the course of the millennia. But there would come a moment, a moment of great importance, when the whole aura assumed a different form and colour. Seen from outside, the earth would then appear in a new light. You would see this event taking place extremely quickly, so that we could say: 'From this moment a fundamental transformation of the earth took place; its aura has changed completely.' What is this moment? It is the moment when upon Golgotha the blood flowed from the wounds of the Redeemer. This moment is an extremely important one, the most important moment in the whole of the earth's evolution. The moment when the blood flows from the wounds of the Redeemer is the same as that in which the aura of the earth reshapes itself. An entirely new power is created, the power which gives the most important impulse to the evolution of earth, for which all that we have considered up to now was only the preparation.

To the chemist, the blood of Golgotha is the same as any other blood, but in reality it is quite different. It signifies that the substance of the blood flows down to the ground, and that its equivalent in the spirit fills the aura of the earth with new impulses and new forces which have significance for the future evolution of mankind. From there the forces which change the earth radiate out, from there they radiate out through human beings. Only a small part of what flowed in at that moment has been realized up to now. Human beings will increasingly learn to understand what the earth has become through that moment of Golgotha, and what human beings can develop towards in that consciousness which they have gained since Atlantis.

What, then, have human beings gained since Atlantis? Two things: ego consciousness and the faculty of sight in the external world. What was previously open to them, the spiritual world, has been closed. These earlier human beings did, indeed, see what was subsequently related by the myths: Wotan-Mercury, Jupiter-Zeus. They saw all these beings at night; they were among them. The door to these spiritual beings has closed. In their place human beings have gained the world which now surrounds them. The spirits have withdrawn from them; all that they were able to see at that time has disappeared. Formerly they saw the divine when they slipped out of the 'snail-shell' of their physical bodies. Now they had to see the divine in a physical body if it was to appear before them. This means nothing less than that we have to receive the divine in a shape which is visible in the body because human consciousness has become adapted to physical vision, and for this reason the divine itself had to assume bodily physical form.

That is why on a single occasion in the evolution of the ages the divine appeared on the earth in a physical body. It had to appear in this form because human beings had advanced to this stage of perception. It had to be presented in this way to their perception so that they could understand it. And all the appearances which had previously taken place at other stages of evolution had to be united in that greatest event in the history of the earth, an event which will throw light on the whole of the future and which we shall now unveil on the basis of the Apocalypse; they were united in that event which had the physical appearance of drops of blood flowing to the ground and the clairvoyant appearance of something rising up which changes the aura of the earth. The force which then flowed in will work together with the earth throughout the whole future. The earth soul, the spirit of the whole earth, was at that time injected with something new. The Christ-principle united with the earth at that time and the earth has become the body of this Christ-principle. So that the statement 'those who eat my bread tread me underfoot' is literally true. When human beings eat the bread of the earth they eat the body of the earth; and this is the body of the earth spirit which, as the spirit of Christ, has been united with the earth since the event on Golgotha. And when human beings walk upon the earth body, they tread this body underfoot. Everything can be comprehended literally if only we are able first of all to understand the text in the right way.

To such a man as the writer of the St John's Gospel, all that he knew, all that he could grasp with his spiritual vision, was a challenge to understand the greatest event in the evolution of the earth. The things he learnt through clairvoyant vision were used by him to understand Christ and his work. It was the intention of the writer of the Apocalypse to use all his esoteric knowledge to explain the event of Golgotha. Whatever he could learn from esoteric science was regarded by him as wisdom serving to help him understand the event which he has placed before us in such a wonderful way.

Notes

1 Cf. Richard Leakey, *The Origin of Humankind* (London 1995), pp. 5–14.

2 Christopher Wills, *The Runaway Brain* (New York 1993).

3 Leakey, pp. 157ff.

4 Using a standard unit of alteration by 1/1000 part per 1000 years, J.Z. Young calculates the rate of evolutionary changes in animals, e.g. early horses, at 60; dinosaurs, at 78; but the rate from *Homo erectus* (Peking man) to modern humanity is not just greater, it seems of a different order, a staggering 620. J.Z. Young, *Introduction to the Study of Humanity* (Oxford and New York 1971), pp. 467–9. On the great plasticity of the early human form, and for some light on the 'gracile' vs. 'robust' forms, cf. Steiner's description in *Occult Science* (London, 1969), p. 199 (new edition, *An Outline of Esoteric Science*, New York 1992). Also p. 35 below.

5 See pp. 23–33.

6 See especially Steiner, *Mystery Knowledge and Mystery Centres* (London 1997) pp. 671ff.

7 See pp. 14–15 of this book.

8 See Scott-Elliot, *The Story of Atlantis and The Lost Lemuria* (repr. London 1968), first map (reproduced here, p. 12); in his second map, South America has moved to join up with that part of the land-mass which will become North America, although the author makes no attempt to explain the nature of the changes.

9 See for instance P. Kearey and F.J. Vine, *Global Tectonics* (Oxford 1996), pp. 46ff, 296ff. For the epochs and life-stages of the Earth

from an anthroposophical perspective, see also Walter Cloos, *The Living Earth* (Sussex 1973).

10 The classical version of the Atlantis myth is contained in Plato's two dialogues, *Timaeus* and *Critias*. Although not mentioning Atlantis by name, almost equally important are the esoteric traditions preserved in the *Book of Enoch* chs. 64–70, 83–9; also II *Enoch* chs. 70–73 relating to the corruption of spiritual knowledge by the 'fallen angels' at the time of the Flood.

11 W. Scott-Elliot, *The Story of Atlantis and The Lost Lemuria* (London 1968). Compare however Steiner's remarks in *Rosicrucian Wisdom* (London 2000), p. 36.

12 Rudolf Steiner has described, from a clairvoyant perspective, not only the shaping of the earth's surface, but the cosmic evolution of our planet in terms of the activity of creative spiritual powers. For an extensive treatment, see Steiner, *Occult Science* (London 1969); for the Spirits of Movement see esp. p. 120. The Spirits of Form are equivalent to the (plural) Elohim ('gods') who in Genesis create the earthly world: *Occult Science*, pp. 174ff; also Steiner, *The Gospel of John* (New York 1962), pp. 50–5.

13 As Rudolf Steiner repeatedly emphasizes, however, the concept of race loses its value in the course of humanity's further development. In times subsequent to Atlantis, one can speak only of different cultures (see e.g. p. 43), not of different racial qualities.

14 In Rudolf Steiner's evolutionary perspective, spiritual diversity (hence individualism, personal freedom, etc.) is the result of a subtle balance of cosmic forces. Not only the creative energy of the divine-spiritual powers is necessary, but also the interaction of this with 'retarding' forces, which have the effect of holding back humanity's evolution too. Two quite separate 'retarding'

powers are characterized in Steiner's spiritual science, though they are related to traditional myths and religious ideas. One is the 'luciferic' tendency; under the sway of this, humanity would resist further change and development, in the comfortable illusion of self-sufficiency. But a more radical retardation is that which Steiner associates with the 'dark' devil Mephistopheles, or the anti-divine Ahriman of Iranian myth. Under the influence of the 'ahrimanic' power, humanity would fail to hold together at all, falling apart and losing autonomy, losing identity. Both Lucifer and Ahriman are necessary to evolution. There had to be an ahrimanic splitting up of the primal divine unity for individual beings to exist—only they must then strive against the ahrimanic and find their way back to God. There had to be a luciferic stage of self-assertion in human development, if the potential for separate being was to be taken up in freedom—only the power of selfhood has to become love for others as individuals like oneself.

The power which enters into earthly, fallen existence to lead the way back to the divine and spiritual is Christ, who thus holds the luciferic and ahrimanic powers in equilibrium, making true freedom and the future evolution of humanity possible. Through Christ the luciferic and ahrimanic forces, destructive in themselves, are made to serve spiritual growth.

15 A reflection of this striving is to be found in the *Laws of Manu*, a code traditionally regarded in India as derived from antediluvian times.

16 'For the present,' wrote Rudolf Steiner in the original edition of this passage, 'it is not permitted to make public communications about the origin of this knowledge and these arts. A passage from the Akashic Record must therefore be omitted here.'

17 The myth of Prometheus, who stole the fire of the gods and gave it to humanity, relates to this betrayal of the Vulcan Mysteries. Cf. Steiner, *The Temple Legend* (London 1985), pp. 36–48.

18 Knowledge of these forms is preserved especially in the Enoch-traditions of 'giants' and demons born to the women who had relations with the fallen, i.e. luciferic, angels.

19 Steiner refers to a prehistoric high culture dating from *c.* 7000 BC.

20 The Zoroastrian traditions which identified the prophet with a figure in historical times actually relate to a reincarnation in the sixth century BC. Cf. Steiner, *The Gospel of Matthew* (London 1965), p. 49. It is widely accepted by scholars nowadays that the original Zarathustra belonged rather to prehistoric times. Steiner dated the archaic Iranian culture to *c.* 5000 BC.

21 The Greeks used the name of their divine messenger Hermes to characterize the Egyptian wisdom-figure, divine and yet human, supposed to have founded their Mysteries. The late Egyptian literature in the name of Hermes still reflects ancient Egyptian wisdom, though of course it is many centuries subsequent to the original Hermes (whom Steiner places *c.* 3000 BC).

22 The direct connection between the inner content of Christianity and the initiation of the ancient Mysteries was forcefully argued by Steiner, *Christianity as Mystical Fact* (New York 1997).

23 The writer of the Apocalypse or Book of Revelation inherited many secrets from the Mysteries, and from the Enoch tradition concerning the luciferic influence on human consciousness. Cf. *Christianity as Mystical Fact*, pp. 136–9.

24 Cf. Steiner, *Genesis: Secrets of the Biblical Creation Story* (London 1982), pp. 120ff.

Sources

This book comprises thematic extracts from the writings and lectures of Rudolf Steiner.

'The Continent of Atlantis' reproduces Steiner, *Cosmic Memory. Atlantis and Lemuria* (New York 1971), pp. 38–41 (translated from GA 11 in the edition of Steiner's original work), and Steiner, *Spiritual Beings in the Heavenly Bodies and in the Kingdoms of Nature* (New York 1992, pp. 93–94 (translated from GA 136 in the edition of Steiner's work).

'The History of Atlantis' reproduces *Cosmic Memory*, pp. 42–58.

'Etheric Technology' reproduces Steiner, *Rosicrucian Esotericism* (New York 1978), pp. 91–9 (translated from GA 109/111 in the edition of Steiner's original work).

'The Divine Messengers' reproduces *Cosmic Memory*, pp. 60–70.

'Atlantean Secret Knowledge' reproduces Steiner, *An Outline of Esoteric Science* (New York 1997) pp. 241–267 (translated from GA 13 in the edition of Steiner's work).

'Concluding Survey' reproduces Steiner, *The Apocalypse of John* (London and New York 1985), pp. 108–19 (translated from GA 104 in the edition of Steiner's original work).

Translations by K.E. Zimmer, D.S. Osmond, C.E. Creeger and J. Collis.

Suggested Further Reading

By Rudolf Steiner:

The Apocalypse of John (London and New York 1985)
Cosmic Memory: Atlantis and Lemuria (New York 1971)
Egyptian Myths and Mysteries (New York 1971)
Genesis: Secrets of the Biblical Creation Story (London 1982)
The Gospel of John (New York 1962)
Mystery Knowledge and Mystery Centres (London 1997)
Occult Science (London 1969). New edition available as *An Outline of Esoteric Science* (New York 1997)
Rosicrucian Esotericism (New York 1978)
Spiritual Foundation of Morality (Vancouver n.d.)
Theosophy of the Rosicrucian (London 1981)

Note Regarding Rudolf Steiner's Lectures

The lectures and addresses contained in this volume have been translated from the German, which is based on stenographic and other recorded texts that were in most cases never seen or revised by the lecturer. Hence, due to human errors in hearing and transcription, they may contain mistakes and faulty passages. Every effort has been made to ensure that this is not the case. Some of the lectures were given to audiences more familiar with anthroposophy; these are the so-called 'private' or 'members' lectures. Other lectures, like the written works, were intended for the general public. The difference between these, as Rudolf Steiner indicates in his *Autobiography*, is twofold. On the one hand, the members' lectures take for granted a background in and commitment to anthroposophy; in the public lectures this was not the case. At the same time, the members' lectures address the concerns and dilemmas of the members, while the public work speaks directly out of Steiner's own understanding of universal needs. Nevertheless, as Rudolf Steiner stresses: 'Nothing was ever said that was not solely the result of my direct experience of the growing content of anthroposophy. There was never any question of concessions to the prejudices and preferences of the members. Whoever reads these privately printed lectures can take them to represent anthroposophy in the fullest sense. Thus it was possible without hesitation — when the complaints in this direction became too persistent — to depart from the custom of circulating this material "For members only". But it must be borne in mind that faulty passages do occur in these reports not revised by myself.' Earlier in the same chapter, he states: 'Had I been able to correct them [the private lectures], the restriction *for members only* would have been unnecessary from the beginning.'

The original German editions on which this text is based were published by Rudolf Steiner Verlag, Dornach, Switzerland in the collected edition (*Gesamtausgabe*, 'GA') of Rudolf Steiner's work. All publications are edited by the Rudolf Steiner Nachlassverwaltung (estate), which wholly owns both Rudolf Steiner Verlag and the Rudolf Steiner Archive.